50 Brazil Nut Bake Recipes for Home

By: Kelly Johnson

Table of Contents

- Brazil Nut Bread
- Brazil Nut Cookies
- Brazil Nut Crusted Chicken
- Brazil Nut Pesto Pasta
- Brazil Nut Salad Dressing
- Brazil Nut Encrusted Fish
- Brazil Nut Milk
- Brazil Nut Energy Bars
- Brazil Nut Brownies
- Brazil Nut Granola
- Brazil Nut Pancakes
- Brazil Nut Pie
- Brazil Nut Cheese
- Brazil Nut Stuffing
- Brazil Nut Hummus
- Brazil Nut Tacos
- Brazil Nut Chocolate Truffles
- Brazil Nut Soup
- Brazil Nut Stir Fry
- Brazil Nut Smoothie
- Brazil Nut Dipping Sauce
- Brazil Nut Risotto
- Brazil Nut Curry
- Brazil Nut Ice Cream
- Brazil Nut Salsa
- Brazil Nut Tapenade
- Brazil Nut Croquettes
- Brazil Nut Cheesecake
- Brazil Nut Torte
- Brazil Nut Fudge
- Brazil Nut Pudding
- Brazil Nut Stuffed Mushrooms
- Brazil Nut Biscotti
- Brazil Nut Quiche
- Brazil Nut Stuffed Peppers
- Brazil Nut Chutney

- Brazil Nut Loaf
- Brazil Nut Risotto
- Brazil Nut Muffins
- Brazil Nut Baked Apples
- Brazil Nut Caramel Sauce
- Brazil Nut Oatmeal
- Brazil Nut Cakes
- Brazil Nut Salad
- Brazil Nut Tiramisu
- Brazil Nut Waffles
- Brazil Nut Bread Pudding
- Brazil Nut Baked Oatmeal
- Brazil Nut Stuffed Dates
- Brazil Nut Trail Mix

Brazil Nut Bread

Ingredients:

- 1 cup Brazil nuts, chopped
- 2 cups all-purpose flour
- 1 teaspoon baking powder
- 1/2 teaspoon baking soda
- 1/2 teaspoon salt
- 1/2 cup unsalted butter, softened
- 1 cup granulated sugar
- 2 large eggs
- 1 teaspoon vanilla extract
- 1 cup plain yogurt or sour cream

Instructions:

1. Preheat Oven and Prepare Pan:
    - Preheat your oven to 350°F (175°C). Grease and flour a 9x5-inch loaf pan.
2. Prepare Brazil Nuts:
    - Chop the Brazil nuts into small pieces. You can toast them lightly in a dry skillet over medium heat for enhanced flavor, if desired.
3. Mix Dry Ingredients:
    - In a medium bowl, whisk together the flour, baking powder, baking soda, and salt.
4. Cream Butter and Sugar:
    - In a large mixing bowl, cream together the softened butter and granulated sugar until light and fluffy.
5. Add Eggs and Vanilla:
    - Beat in the eggs one at a time, then add the vanilla extract, mixing until well combined.
6. Alternate Adding Dry and Wet Ingredients:
    - Gradually add the flour mixture to the creamed butter and sugar mixture, alternating with the yogurt or sour cream. Start and end with the flour mixture, mixing until just combined.
7. Fold in Brazil Nuts:
    - Gently fold in the chopped Brazil nuts until evenly distributed throughout the batter.
8. Bake:
    - Pour the batter into the prepared loaf pan and smooth the top with a spatula.
    - Bake in the preheated oven for 50-60 minutes, or until a toothpick inserted into the center comes out clean.
9. Cool:

- Allow the Brazil Nut Bread to cool in the pan for 10-15 minutes before removing it from the pan and transferring it to a wire rack to cool completely.
10. Serve:
    - Slice and serve the Brazil Nut Bread plain, with butter, or with your favorite spread. Enjoy!

This Brazil Nut Bread is moist, flavorful, and perfect for breakfast or as a snack. The chopped Brazil nuts add a delightful crunch and nutty flavor to every bite.

Brazil Nut Cookies

Ingredients:

- 1 cup Brazil nuts, finely chopped
- 1 cup unsalted butter, softened
- 1 cup granulated sugar
- 1 cup brown sugar, packed
- 2 large eggs
- 2 teaspoons vanilla extract
- 2 cups all-purpose flour
- 1 teaspoon baking soda
- 1/2 teaspoon baking powder
- 1/2 teaspoon salt
- Optional: 1 cup chocolate chips or chopped dark chocolate (for chocolate chip Brazil nut cookies)

Instructions:

1. Preheat Oven:
    - Preheat your oven to 350°F (175°C). Line baking sheets with parchment paper or silicone baking mats.
2. Prepare Brazil Nuts:
    - Finely chop the Brazil nuts using a food processor or by hand. Set aside.
3. Cream Butter and Sugars:
    - In a large bowl, cream together the softened butter, granulated sugar, and brown sugar until light and fluffy.
4. Add Eggs and Vanilla:
    - Beat in the eggs, one at a time, until well combined. Add the vanilla extract and mix until smooth.
5. Combine Dry Ingredients:
    - In a separate bowl, whisk together the flour, baking soda, baking powder, and salt.
6. Mix Wet and Dry Ingredients:
    - Gradually add the dry ingredients to the wet ingredients, mixing until just combined. Avoid overmixing.
7. Fold in Brazil Nuts (and Chocolate, if using):
    - Gently fold in the finely chopped Brazil nuts (and chocolate chips or chopped chocolate, if desired) until evenly distributed throughout the cookie dough.
8. Shape Cookies:
    - Drop rounded tablespoons of cookie dough onto the prepared baking sheets, spacing them about 2 inches apart.
9. Bake:

- Bake in the preheated oven for 10-12 minutes, or until the edges are lightly golden brown. The centers may still look slightly soft, but they will continue to firm up as they cool.
10. Cool and Enjoy:
    - Allow the cookies to cool on the baking sheets for 5 minutes before transferring them to wire racks to cool completely.
11. Store:
    - Once completely cooled, store the Brazil Nut Cookies in an airtight container at room temperature for up to one week.

These Brazil Nut Cookies are perfect for any occasion and are sure to be a hit with their rich nutty flavor and chewy texture. Enjoy them with a glass of milk or a cup of coffee for a delightful treat!

Brazil Nut Crusted Chicken

Ingredients:

- 4 boneless, skinless chicken breasts
- 1 cup Brazil nuts, finely chopped
- 1/2 cup breadcrumbs (plain or seasoned)
- 1/4 cup grated Parmesan cheese
- 1 teaspoon dried thyme
- 1/2 teaspoon garlic powder
- Salt and pepper, to taste
- 2 large eggs
- 2 tablespoons olive oil

Instructions:

1. Preheat Oven:
    - Preheat your oven to 375°F (190°C). Line a baking sheet with parchment paper or foil.
2. Prepare Chicken:
    - Season the chicken breasts with salt and pepper on both sides.
3. Prepare Coating Mixture:
    - In a shallow bowl or dish, combine the finely chopped Brazil nuts, breadcrumbs, grated Parmesan cheese, dried thyme, garlic powder, salt, and pepper. Mix well to combine.
4. Coat Chicken:
    - In another shallow bowl, whisk the eggs until well beaten.
    - Dip each chicken breast into the beaten eggs, coating both sides thoroughly.
5. Dredge in Nut Mixture:
    - Press each egg-coated chicken breast into the Brazil nut mixture, ensuring the nuts adhere to the chicken on both sides. Press gently to coat evenly.
6. Cook Chicken:
    - In a large oven-safe skillet or frying pan, heat the olive oil over medium-high heat.
    - Once hot, add the coated chicken breasts to the skillet and cook for 3-4 minutes on each side, or until the nuts are golden brown and the chicken is cooked through.
7. Finish in Oven:
    - Transfer the skillet to the preheated oven and bake for an additional 10-15 minutes, or until the internal temperature of the chicken reaches 165°F (75°C) and the coating is crispy.
8. Serve:
    - Remove from the oven and let the Brazil Nut Crusted Chicken rest for a few minutes before slicing and serving. Optionally, garnish with fresh herbs or a squeeze of lemon juice.

9. Enjoy:
    - Serve the Brazil Nut Crusted Chicken hot, accompanied by your favorite sides such as roasted vegetables, salad, or rice. The crunchy Brazil nut crust adds a delightful texture and nutty flavor to the tender chicken breasts.

This Brazil Nut Crusted Chicken recipe is simple to prepare and makes for an impressive main dish that is both flavorful and satisfying. Adjust the seasoning and thickness of the nut coating to suit your taste preferences.

Brazil Nut Pesto Pasta

Ingredients:

For the Brazil Nut Pesto:

- 1 cup Brazil nuts, toasted
- 2 cups fresh basil leaves, packed
- 2 cloves garlic, minced
- 1/2 cup grated Parmesan cheese
- 1/2 cup extra virgin olive oil
- Juice of 1 lemon
- Salt and pepper, to taste

For the Pasta:

- 12 ounces (about 340g) pasta of your choice (such as spaghetti, fettuccine, or penne)
- Cherry tomatoes, halved (optional)
- Fresh basil leaves, for garnish
- Grated Parmesan cheese, for serving

Instructions:

1. Toast Brazil Nuts:
    - Preheat your oven to 350°F (175°C). Spread the Brazil nuts in a single layer on a baking sheet and toast in the oven for about 8-10 minutes, or until fragrant and lightly golden. Allow them to cool slightly.
2. Make Brazil Nut Pesto:
    - In a food processor, combine the toasted Brazil nuts, basil leaves, minced garlic, grated Parmesan cheese, and lemon juice. Pulse several times to chop the ingredients.
3. Add Olive Oil:
    - With the food processor running, gradually drizzle in the olive oil until the pesto reaches a smooth and creamy consistency. Stop to scrape down the sides of the food processor as needed.
4. Season:
    - Taste the Brazil Nut Pesto and season with salt and pepper to taste. Adjust the consistency with more olive oil if necessary.
5. Cook Pasta:
    - Cook the pasta according to the package instructions in a large pot of salted boiling water until al dente. Reserve about 1 cup of pasta cooking water before draining.
6. Combine Pasta and Pesto:

- In a large mixing bowl, toss the cooked pasta with the prepared Brazil Nut Pesto until well coated. Use some of the reserved pasta cooking water to thin out the pesto sauce as needed.
7. Serve:
    - Divide the Brazil Nut Pesto Pasta among serving plates. Garnish with halved cherry tomatoes (if using), fresh basil leaves, and grated Parmesan cheese.
8. Enjoy:
    - Serve the Brazil Nut Pesto Pasta immediately while warm. Enjoy the nutty, herbaceous flavors of the pesto with your favorite pasta shape!

This Brazil Nut Pesto Pasta is a delightful and satisfying dish that can be served as a main course or as a side dish. The homemade pesto with Brazil nuts adds a unique twist to classic pasta dishes, making it perfect for any occasion. Adjust the quantities of ingredients to suit your taste preferences and enjoy a taste of freshness and nuttiness in every bite.

Brazil Nut Salad Dressing

Ingredients:

- 1/2 cup Brazil nuts, toasted
- 1/4 cup extra virgin olive oil
- 1/4 cup water
- 2 tablespoons apple cider vinegar or lemon juice
- 1 clove garlic, minced
- 1 teaspoon Dijon mustard
- 1 teaspoon honey or maple syrup (optional, for sweetness)
- Salt and pepper, to taste

Instructions:

1. Toast Brazil Nuts:
    - Preheat your oven to 350°F (175°C). Spread the Brazil nuts in a single layer on a baking sheet and toast for about 8-10 minutes, or until fragrant and lightly golden. Allow them to cool slightly.
2. Prepare Dressing:
    - In a food processor or blender, combine the toasted Brazil nuts, olive oil, water, apple cider vinegar or lemon juice, minced garlic, Dijon mustard, and honey or maple syrup (if using).
3. Blend Until Smooth:
    - Blend the ingredients until smooth and creamy. You may need to scrape down the sides of the food processor or blender a few times to ensure all ingredients are well incorporated.
4. Season:
    - Taste the dressing and season with salt and pepper to taste. Adjust the acidity with more vinegar or lemon juice if desired.
5. Adjust Consistency:
    - If the dressing is too thick, you can thin it out with a little more water or olive oil until you reach your desired consistency.
6. Serve:
    - Transfer the Brazil Nut Salad Dressing to a jar or container with a tight-fitting lid. Refrigerate for at least 30 minutes to allow the flavors to meld together before serving.
7. Enjoy:
    - Drizzle the Brazil Nut Salad Dressing over your favorite salads just before serving. It pairs well with mixed greens, spinach, kale, or any combination of fresh vegetables. Optionally, garnish with additional toasted Brazil nuts or fresh herbs.

This creamy Brazil Nut Salad Dressing adds a nutty richness and depth of flavor to salads, making it a healthy and delicious choice for dressing up your greens. Store any leftover dressing in the refrigerator for up to one week.

Brazil Nut Encrusted Fish

Ingredients:

- 4 fillets of white fish (such as tilapia, cod, or halibut)
- 1 cup Brazil nuts, finely chopped or ground
- 1/2 cup breadcrumbs (plain or seasoned)
- 1/4 cup grated Parmesan cheese
- 1 teaspoon dried thyme
- 1/2 teaspoon garlic powder
- Salt and pepper, to taste
- 2 tablespoons Dijon mustard or mayonnaise
- Lemon wedges, for serving

Instructions:

1. Preheat Oven:
    - Preheat your oven to 400°F (200°C). Line a baking sheet with parchment paper or foil.
2. Prepare the Nut Mixture:
    - In a shallow bowl or dish, combine the finely chopped or ground Brazil nuts, breadcrumbs, grated Parmesan cheese, dried thyme, garlic powder, salt, and pepper. Mix well to combine.
3. Coat the Fish:
    - Pat dry the fish fillets with paper towels. Season both sides of each fillet with salt and pepper.
    - Brush each fillet with Dijon mustard or mayonnaise on one side.
4. Apply Nut Crust:
    - Press the mustard or mayonnaise-coated side of each fillet into the Brazil nut mixture, ensuring the nuts adhere to the fish evenly and coat well.
5. Bake the Fish:
    - Place the coated fish fillets on the prepared baking sheet, nut-side up.
    - Bake in the preheated oven for 12-15 minutes, or until the fish is cooked through and the nut crust is golden brown and crispy.
6. Serve:
    - Remove from the oven and let the Brazil Nut Encrusted Fish rest for a few minutes before serving.
    - Serve hot, garnished with lemon wedges for squeezing over the fish.
7. Enjoy:
    - Enjoy the Brazil Nut Encrusted Fish as a flavorful and nutritious main dish. Serve alongside your favorite vegetables, salad, or rice for a complete meal.

This Brazil Nut Encrusted Fish recipe is simple yet elegant, making it perfect for both weeknight dinners and special occasions. The crunchy nut crust adds texture and flavor, complementing the tender fish beautifully. Adjust the seasoning and type of fish according to your preference for a delightful dining experience.

Brazil Nut Milk

Ingredients:

- 1 cup raw Brazil nuts
- 4 cups water (plus more for soaking)
- Optional sweeteners or flavorings: honey, maple syrup, vanilla extract, dates, cinnamon (adjust to taste)

Instructions:

1. Soak the Brazil Nuts:
    - Place the Brazil nuts in a bowl and cover them with water. Let them soak for at least 4 hours or overnight. Soaking helps to soften the nuts and makes them easier to blend.
2. Rinse and Drain:
    - After soaking, drain and rinse the Brazil nuts thoroughly under cold water.
3. Blend:
    - In a blender, combine the soaked Brazil nuts and 4 cups of fresh water. If you prefer a creamier milk, use less water; for a thinner consistency, add more water.
    - Optional: Add sweeteners or flavorings such as honey, maple syrup, vanilla extract, dates, or cinnamon to taste.
4. Blend Until Smooth:
    - Blend on high speed for about 1-2 minutes until the mixture is smooth and creamy.
5. Strain (optional):
    - For a smoother texture, strain the Brazil nut milk through a nut milk bag, cheesecloth, or fine mesh sieve into a large bowl or pitcher. Squeeze or press the pulp to extract as much liquid as possible. (Note: Alternatively, you can skip straining for a more rustic texture.)
6. Store:
    - Transfer the Brazil nut milk to a sealed container or glass bottle and refrigerate. It will keep for about 3-4 days. Shake well before each use, as natural separation may occur.
7. Enjoy:
    - Use Brazil Nut Milk in smoothies, coffee, tea, cereal, or any recipe that calls for milk. It's also delicious on its own as a refreshing drink.

Tips:

- Variations: Experiment with different flavorings like cocoa powder for chocolate milk or matcha powder for a green tea latte.
- Nutritional Benefits: Brazil nut milk is rich in healthy fats, protein, vitamins, and minerals, including selenium, which is important for immune function and thyroid health.

- Storage: Store any leftover Brazil nut pulp in the freezer to use in baking or cooking recipes.

Making Brazil Nut Milk at home allows you to control the ingredients and customize the flavor to your preference. Enjoy this dairy-free alternative as part of a healthy and nutritious diet!

Brazil Nut Energy Bars

Ingredients:

- 1 cup Brazil nuts
- 1 cup pitted dates
- 1/2 cup rolled oats
- 1/4 cup shredded coconut (unsweetened)
- 2 tablespoons chia seeds
- 2 tablespoons honey or maple syrup (optional, for sweetness)
- 1/2 teaspoon vanilla extract
- Pinch of salt

Instructions:

1. Prepare Brazil Nuts:
    - If your Brazil nuts are not already chopped, roughly chop them with a knife or pulse them in a food processor until finely chopped. Set aside.
2. Process Dates:
    - In a food processor, blend the pitted dates until they form a sticky paste-like consistency.
3. Combine Ingredients:
    - Add the chopped Brazil nuts, rolled oats, shredded coconut, chia seeds, honey or maple syrup (if using), vanilla extract, and a pinch of salt to the food processor with the dates.
4. Blend Until Combined:
    - Pulse or blend the mixture in the food processor until everything is well combined and forms a sticky dough-like texture. It should stick together when pressed between your fingers.
5. Press into Pan:
    - Line a baking dish or square pan with parchment paper or plastic wrap for easy removal. Transfer the mixture into the pan and press it firmly and evenly with your hands or the back of a spoon.
6. Chill:
    - Place the pan in the refrigerator for at least 1-2 hours to allow the bars to firm up and set.
7. Cut into Bars:
    - Once chilled and firm, remove the mixture from the pan using the edges of the parchment paper or plastic wrap. Use a sharp knife to cut the mixture into bars or squares of your desired size.
8. Store:
    - Store the Brazil Nut Energy Bars in an airtight container in the refrigerator for up to one week. For longer storage, individually wrap the bars in plastic wrap or parchment paper and store them in the freezer.
9. Enjoy:

- Grab a Brazil Nut Energy Bar as a quick and nutritious snack on the go, or enjoy it as a pre- or post-workout fuel. These bars are packed with protein, healthy fats, fiber, and natural sweetness from the dates.

This recipe is versatile, so feel free to customize it by adding other ingredients such as cocoa powder, dried fruits, or protein powder to suit your taste preferences. Brazil Nut Energy Bars are a satisfying and wholesome snack option that provides sustained energy and nutrition.

Brazil Nut Brownies

Ingredients:

- 1/2 cup unsalted butter
- 8 ounces (about 225g) dark chocolate (60-70% cocoa), coarsely chopped
- 1 cup granulated sugar
- 3 large eggs
- 1 teaspoon vanilla extract
- 1/2 cup all-purpose flour
- 1/4 teaspoon salt
- 1/2 cup Brazil nuts, chopped

Instructions:

1. Preheat Oven and Prepare Pan:
    - Preheat your oven to 350°F (175°C). Grease and line an 8x8-inch baking pan with parchment paper, leaving an overhang on the sides for easy removal.
2. Melt Butter and Chocolate:
    - In a medium saucepan, melt the butter and chopped dark chocolate over low heat, stirring frequently, until smooth and melted. Remove from heat and let cool slightly.
3. Mix Sugar, Eggs, and Vanilla:
    - In a large mixing bowl, whisk together the granulated sugar, eggs, and vanilla extract until well combined.
4. Combine Chocolate Mixture:
    - Gradually pour the melted chocolate mixture into the sugar and egg mixture, stirring until smooth.
5. Add Flour and Salt:
    - Sift in the all-purpose flour and salt into the chocolate mixture. Stir until just combined; do not overmix.
6. Fold in Chopped Brazil Nuts:
    - Gently fold in the chopped Brazil nuts until evenly distributed throughout the brownie batter.
7. Bake:
    - Pour the brownie batter into the prepared baking pan, spreading it evenly with a spatula.
8. Bake the Brownies:
    - Bake in the preheated oven for 25-30 minutes, or until a toothpick inserted into the center comes out with a few moist crumbs attached. Be careful not to overbake.
9. Cool and Slice:
    - Remove the brownies from the oven and let them cool completely in the pan on a wire rack. Once cooled, lift the brownies out of the pan using the parchment

paper overhang and transfer them to a cutting board. Cut into squares or rectangles.
10. Serve:
    - Serve the Brazil Nut Brownies at room temperature. Optionally, dust with powdered sugar or serve with a scoop of ice cream for a decadent dessert.

These Brazil Nut Brownies are rich, fudgy, and packed with a delightful crunch from the chopped Brazil nuts. They are perfect for chocolate lovers and make a wonderful treat for any occasion. Enjoy these brownies with a glass of milk or your favorite hot beverage!

Brazil Nut Granola

Ingredients:

- 3 cups old-fashioned rolled oats
- 1 cup Brazil nuts, chopped
- 1/2 cup shredded coconut (unsweetened)
- 1/2 cup raw honey or maple syrup
- 1/4 cup coconut oil, melted
- 1 teaspoon vanilla extract
- 1/2 teaspoon ground cinnamon
- 1/4 teaspoon salt
- 1 cup dried fruit (optional, such as raisins, cranberries, or chopped apricots)

Instructions:

1. Preheat Oven:
   - Preheat your oven to 300°F (150°C). Line a large baking sheet with parchment paper or a silicone baking mat.
2. Mix Dry Ingredients:
   - In a large bowl, combine the rolled oats, chopped Brazil nuts, shredded coconut, ground cinnamon, and salt. Mix well to combine.
3. Prepare Wet Ingredients:
   - In a separate microwave-safe bowl or small saucepan, melt the coconut oil. Add the honey or maple syrup and vanilla extract to the melted coconut oil. Stir until well combined.
4. Combine Dry and Wet Ingredients:
   - Pour the melted coconut oil mixture over the dry ingredients in the large bowl. Stir until the oats and nuts are evenly coated with the honey/oil mixture.
5. Spread on Baking Sheet:
   - Spread the granola mixture evenly onto the prepared baking sheet. Use a spatula or the back of a spoon to press it down slightly.
6. Bake:
   - Bake in the preheated oven for 30-35 minutes, stirring halfway through. The granola should be golden brown and crisp when done.
7. Add Dried Fruit (Optional):
   - If using dried fruit, add it to the granola immediately after removing it from the oven. Mix well to combine.
8. Cool Completely:
   - Allow the Brazil Nut Granola to cool completely on the baking sheet. It will crisp up further as it cools.
9. Store:
   - Once completely cooled, transfer the granola to an airtight container or glass jar for storage. It will keep well at room temperature for up to 2 weeks.
10. Serve and Enjoy:

- Serve the Brazil Nut Granola with milk or yogurt for breakfast, or enjoy it as a nutritious snack on its own. You can also use it as a topping for smoothie bowls or ice cream.

This homemade Brazil Nut Granola is customizable, so feel free to adjust the sweetness, spices, or add other nuts and seeds according to your taste preferences. It's a delicious and wholesome way to start your day or refuel during a busy afternoon!

Brazil Nut Pancakes

Ingredients:

- 1 cup all-purpose flour
- 1/2 cup Brazil nuts, finely ground (you can use a food processor)
- 2 tablespoons granulated sugar
- 2 teaspoons baking powder
- 1/2 teaspoon baking soda
- 1/4 teaspoon salt
- 1 cup milk (dairy or plant-based)
- 1 large egg
- 2 tablespoons unsalted butter, melted
- 1 teaspoon vanilla extract

Instructions:

1. Prepare Brazil Nuts:
    - Start by grinding the Brazil nuts finely using a food processor. Make sure they are ground into a fine meal-like consistency.
2. Mix Dry Ingredients:
    - In a large bowl, whisk together the all-purpose flour, finely ground Brazil nuts, granulated sugar, baking powder, baking soda, and salt until well combined.
3. Combine Wet Ingredients:
    - In a separate bowl, whisk together the milk, egg, melted butter, and vanilla extract until smooth.
4. Combine Wet and Dry Ingredients:
    - Pour the wet ingredients into the bowl with the dry ingredients. Stir gently with a spatula or wooden spoon until just combined. Be careful not to overmix; a few lumps are okay.
5. Rest the Batter:
    - Let the pancake batter rest for about 5-10 minutes. This allows the baking powder and baking soda to activate and helps create fluffier pancakes.
6. Cook Pancakes:
    - Heat a non-stick griddle or skillet over medium heat. Lightly grease the surface with butter or cooking spray.
    - Pour 1/4 cup of batter onto the hot griddle for each pancake. Cook until bubbles form on the surface of the pancakes and the edges look set, about 2-3 minutes.
7. Flip and Cook:
    - Carefully flip each pancake with a spatula and cook on the other side until golden brown, about 1-2 minutes more.
8. Serve:
    - Transfer the cooked Brazil Nut Pancakes to a serving plate. Serve warm with your favorite toppings such as maple syrup, fresh berries, whipped cream, or additional chopped Brazil nuts.

9. Enjoy:
    - Enjoy these delicious Brazil Nut Pancakes as a delightful breakfast or brunch treat!

This recipe yields fluffy pancakes with a nutty flavor from the ground Brazil nuts. It's a wonderful way to add a nutritious twist to your morning pancakes and enjoy the unique taste of Brazil nuts.

Brazil Nut Pie

Ingredients:

For the Crust:

- 1 1/4 cups all-purpose flour
- 1/4 teaspoon salt
- 1/2 cup unsalted butter, chilled and diced
- 3-4 tablespoons ice water

For the Filling:

- 1 cup Brazil nuts, finely chopped
- 1 cup light brown sugar, packed
- 1/2 cup corn syrup (light or dark)
- 1/4 cup unsalted butter, melted
- 3 large eggs, beaten
- 1 teaspoon vanilla extract
- 1/4 teaspoon salt

Instructions:

1. Prepare the Crust:
     - In a food processor, pulse the flour and salt together to combine. Add the chilled, diced butter and pulse until the mixture resembles coarse crumbs.
     - Gradually add the ice water, 1 tablespoon at a time, pulsing until the dough just begins to come together. You may not need all the water.
     - Turn the dough out onto a lightly floured surface and gather it into a ball. Flatten into a disk, wrap in plastic wrap, and refrigerate for at least 30 minutes.
2. Preheat Oven:
     - Preheat your oven to 350°F (175°C).
3. Roll Out the Crust:
     - On a lightly floured surface, roll out the chilled dough into a circle about 12 inches in diameter. Transfer the dough to a 9-inch pie dish. Trim and crimp the edges as desired.
4. Prepare the Filling:
     - In a large mixing bowl, combine the chopped Brazil nuts, brown sugar, corn syrup, melted butter, beaten eggs, vanilla extract, and salt. Mix well until all ingredients are thoroughly combined.
5. Assemble and Bake:
     - Pour the filling into the prepared pie crust. Spread it evenly with a spatula.
6. Bake the Pie:
     - Bake in the preheated oven for 50-60 minutes, or until the filling is set and slightly puffed, and the crust is golden brown.

- If the edges of the crust begin to brown too quickly, cover them loosely with foil halfway through baking.
7. **Cool and Serve:**
    - Remove the pie from the oven and allow it to cool completely on a wire rack before slicing and serving.
    - Serve slices of Brazilian Nut Pie at room temperature or slightly warmed, optionally topped with whipped cream or a scoop of vanilla ice cream.
8. **Enjoy:**
    - Enjoy the rich, nutty flavors of Brazilian Nut Pie as a delicious dessert for any occasion!

This Brazilian Nut Pie recipe yields a luscious and indulgent dessert that showcases the unique flavor and texture of Brazil nuts. It's perfect for holidays, special gatherings, or whenever you're craving a sweet treat with a nutty twist.

Brazil Nut Cheese

Ingredients:

- 1 cup raw Brazil nuts
- 2 tablespoons nutritional yeast
- 2 tablespoons lemon juice
- 1-2 cloves garlic, minced (optional)
- 1/2 teaspoon salt, or to taste
- Water, as needed for blending
- Fresh herbs (such as thyme or rosemary), chopped (optional, for garnish)

Instructions:

1. Soak the Brazil Nuts:
    - Place the Brazil nuts in a bowl and cover them with water. Allow them to soak for at least 4 hours or overnight. Soaking helps to soften the nuts and make them easier to blend.
2. Drain and Rinse:
    - After soaking, drain and rinse the Brazil nuts thoroughly under cold water.
3. Blend Ingredients:
    - In a food processor or high-speed blender, combine the soaked Brazil nuts, nutritional yeast, lemon juice, minced garlic (if using), and salt.
4. Blend Until Smooth:
    - Begin blending the ingredients, adding water gradually as needed to achieve a smooth and creamy consistency. Aim for a texture similar to soft cheese.
5. Adjust Seasoning:
    - Taste the Brazil Nut Cheese and adjust the seasoning as desired, adding more salt or lemon juice to suit your taste.
6. Transfer and Chill (Optional):
    - If you prefer a firmer cheese, you can transfer the mixture to a cheesecloth-lined strainer set over a bowl. Fold the cheesecloth over the top and place a weight (such as a can) on top to gently press out excess moisture. Refrigerate for a few hours or overnight.
7. Serve:
    - Once chilled (if desired), transfer the Brazil Nut Cheese to a serving bowl. Garnish with fresh chopped herbs if using.
8. Enjoy:
    - Serve the Brazil Nut Cheese as a spread on crackers or bread, as a dip for vegetables, or incorporate it into recipes where you would use dairy cheese.

Tips:

- Variations: Experiment with adding different herbs and spices to customize the flavor of your Brazil Nut Cheese.

- Storage: Store any leftover Brazil Nut Cheese in an airtight container in the refrigerator for up to one week.

Brazil Nut Cheese is a creamy and nutritious alternative to dairy cheese, rich in healthy fats and protein from the nuts. It's versatile and can be enjoyed in various ways, making it a great addition to a plant-based diet or for anyone looking to explore dairy-free options.

Brazil Nut Stuffing

Ingredients:

- 8 cups bread cubes (about 1 loaf of bread, cubed and dried)
- 1 cup Brazil nuts, chopped
- 1 large onion, diced
- 3 celery stalks, diced
- 4 cloves garlic, minced
- 1/2 cup unsalted butter or olive oil
- 1 cup vegetable or chicken broth
- 2 tablespoons fresh parsley, chopped
- 1 tablespoon fresh sage, chopped (or 1 teaspoon dried sage)
- 1 tablespoon fresh thyme leaves (or 1 teaspoon dried thyme)
- Salt and pepper, to taste

Instructions:

1. Prepare Bread Cubes:
    - If your bread cubes are not already dried, spread them out on a baking sheet and let them sit at room temperature for a few hours or bake them in a low oven (300°F or 150°C) for about 15-20 minutes until they are dried and slightly crisp.
2. Sauté Vegetables:
    - In a large skillet or pan, melt the butter or heat the olive oil over medium heat. Add the diced onion, celery, and minced garlic. Sauté until the vegetables are softened and translucent, about 5-7 minutes.
3. Combine Ingredients:
    - In a large mixing bowl, combine the dried bread cubes, chopped Brazil nuts, sautéed vegetables, chopped parsley, sage, and thyme. Season with salt and pepper to taste.
4. Moisten with Broth:
    - Pour the vegetable or chicken broth over the bread mixture. Stir well to combine, ensuring that the bread cubes absorb the liquid evenly. Add more broth if needed until the stuffing is moist but not soggy.
5. Bake or Stuff:
    - Transfer the Brazil Nut Stuffing to a greased baking dish if baking separately, or use it to stuff poultry such as chicken or turkey if preferred.
6. Bake (if baking separately):
    - Cover the baking dish with foil and bake in a preheated oven at 350°F (175°C) for 30 minutes. Remove the foil and bake for an additional 10-15 minutes until the top is golden brown and crispy.
7. Serve:
    - Serve the Brazil Nut Stuffing warm as a side dish alongside your favorite roast, poultry, or as part of a festive meal.

Tips:

- Variations: Add dried fruits such as cranberries or apricots for a sweeter twist, or incorporate cooked sausage or bacon for a richer flavor.
- Make-Ahead: Prepare the stuffing in advance and refrigerate it overnight. Bake it just before serving to save time on the day of your meal.

This Brazil Nut Stuffing recipe offers a delicious combination of crunchy Brazil nuts, flavorful herbs, and savory vegetables, making it a delightful addition to any holiday table or special occasion meal.

Brazil Nut Hummus

Ingredients:

- 1 cup cooked chickpeas (or 1 can, drained and rinsed)
- 1/2 cup Brazil nuts, raw or lightly toasted
- 1/4 cup tahini (sesame seed paste)
- 2 cloves garlic, minced
- 1/4 cup fresh lemon juice (about 1-2 lemons)
- 1/4 cup water (more as needed)
- 2 tablespoons extra virgin olive oil
- 1/2 teaspoon ground cumin
- 1/2 teaspoon salt, or to taste
- Freshly ground black pepper, to taste
- Optional toppings: olive oil, paprika, chopped fresh herbs (parsley, cilantro)

Instructions:

1. Prepare Brazil Nuts:
    - If using raw Brazil nuts, you may lightly toast them in a dry skillet over medium heat for a few minutes until fragrant. Let them cool before using.
2. Blend Ingredients:
    - In a food processor, combine the cooked chickpeas, Brazil nuts, tahini, minced garlic, lemon juice, water, olive oil, ground cumin, salt, and black pepper.
3. Blend Until Smooth:
    - Process the mixture until smooth and creamy, scraping down the sides of the bowl as needed. If the hummus is too thick, add more water, 1 tablespoon at a time, until you reach your desired consistency.
4. Adjust Seasoning:
    - Taste the Brazil Nut Hummus and adjust the seasoning if needed, adding more salt, lemon juice, or cumin according to your preference.
5. Serve:
    - Transfer the Brazil Nut Hummus to a serving bowl. Drizzle with a little extra virgin olive oil and sprinkle with paprika for color. Garnish with chopped fresh herbs if desired.
6. Enjoy:
    - Serve the Brazil Nut Hummus with pita bread, crackers, vegetable sticks, or use it as a spread or dip for sandwiches and wraps.

Tips:

- Variations: For added flavor, you can incorporate roasted red peppers, sun-dried tomatoes, or herbs like basil or parsley into the hummus.
- Storage: Store leftover Brazil Nut Hummus in an airtight container in the refrigerator for up to 5 days. Stir well before serving.

This Brazil Nut Hummus recipe offers a creamy texture with a nutty flavor twist, perfect for parties, snacks, or as a healthy addition to your meals. Enjoy experimenting with different variations and toppings to suit your taste!

Brazil Nut Tacos

Ingredients:

For the Brazil Nut "Meat":

- 1 cup Brazil nuts
- 1 tablespoon olive oil
- 1 small onion, finely chopped
- 2 cloves garlic, minced
- 1 teaspoon ground cumin
- 1 teaspoon chili powder
- 1/2 teaspoon smoked paprika
- Salt and pepper, to taste
- 1/4 cup vegetable broth or water

For the Tacos:

- Corn or flour tortillas
- Toppings: Shredded lettuce, diced tomatoes, sliced avocado, salsa, cilantro, lime wedges, etc.

Instructions:

1. Prepare Brazil Nut "Meat":
   - In a food processor, pulse the Brazil nuts until they are finely chopped but not powdered. Set aside.
2. Sauté Onion and Garlic:
   - Heat olive oil in a large skillet over medium heat. Add the finely chopped onion and minced garlic. Sauté until the onion is translucent and fragrant, about 3-4 minutes.
3. Cook the "Meat":
   - Add the chopped Brazil nuts to the skillet with the sautéed onion and garlic. Stir in the ground cumin, chili powder, smoked paprika, salt, and pepper. Cook, stirring frequently, for about 5-7 minutes until the Brazil nuts are toasted and aromatic.
4. Add Liquid:
   - Pour in the vegetable broth or water to deglaze the skillet, scraping up any browned bits from the bottom. Cook for an additional 2-3 minutes until the liquid is absorbed and the "meat" mixture is well combined and heated through. Adjust seasoning to taste.
5. Assemble Tacos:
   - Warm the tortillas in a dry skillet or oven until soft and pliable.
   - Spoon the Brazil Nut "meat" mixture into the warmed tortillas.
6. Add Toppings:

- Top each taco with shredded lettuce, diced tomatoes, sliced avocado, salsa, cilantro, or any other toppings you prefer.
7. Serve:
    - Serve the Brazil Nut Tacos immediately, garnished with lime wedges for squeezing over the tacos.

Tips:

- Variations: Customize your tacos with additional toppings such as cheese (dairy or vegan), sour cream (dairy or vegan), pickled jalapeños, or a drizzle of hot sauce.
- Storage: Store any leftover Brazil Nut "meat" in an airtight container in the refrigerator for up to 3 days. Reheat gently before using.

These Brazil Nut Tacos offer a delicious and satisfying alternative to traditional meat-based tacos, showcasing the unique flavor and texture of Brazil nuts. They are perfect for a vegetarian or vegan meal option that's full of flavor and nutrition.

Brazil Nut Chocolate Truffles

Ingredients:

- 1 cup Brazil nuts
- 8 ounces (about 225g) dark chocolate, finely chopped
- 1/2 cup heavy cream (or coconut cream for a dairy-free option)
- 1 teaspoon vanilla extract
- Pinch of salt
- Cocoa powder, powdered sugar, or finely chopped nuts for coating (optional)

Instructions:

1. Toast Brazil Nuts (Optional):
    - If desired, toast the Brazil nuts in a dry skillet over medium heat for a few minutes until lightly browned and fragrant. Let them cool completely before using.
2. Grind Brazil Nuts:
    - Place the Brazil nuts in a food processor and pulse until finely ground. You want a fine meal-like texture but not completely powdered.
3. Prepare Chocolate:
    - Place the finely chopped dark chocolate in a heatproof bowl.
4. Heat Cream:
    - In a small saucepan, heat the heavy cream (or coconut cream) until it just begins to simmer. Remove from heat immediately.
5. Make Ganache:
    - Pour the hot cream over the chopped chocolate. Let it sit for a minute to soften the chocolate, then stir gently until the chocolate is melted and smooth.
6. Add Flavorings:
    - Stir in the vanilla extract and a pinch of salt.
7. Combine with Ground Nuts:
    - Add the ground Brazil nuts to the chocolate ganache mixture. Stir well until fully incorporated.
8. Chill the Mixture:
    - Cover the bowl with plastic wrap and refrigerate the mixture until firm, at least 2 hours or overnight.
9. Shape Truffles:
    - Once chilled and firm, scoop out tablespoon-sized portions of the chocolate mixture and roll them into balls using your hands. Place the rolled truffles on a parchment-lined baking sheet.
10. Coat Truffles (Optional):
    - Roll the truffles in cocoa powder, powdered sugar, or finely chopped nuts to coat them evenly. You can also leave them plain if desired.
11. Chill Again (Optional):

- For best texture, chill the coated truffles in the refrigerator for another 30 minutes to set.
12. Serve:
    - Serve the Brazil Nut Chocolate Truffles at room temperature. Store any leftovers in an airtight container in the refrigerator for up to 1 week.

Tips:

- Variations: Experiment with different coatings such as melted chocolate for a double chocolate coating or crushed freeze-dried berries for a fruity twist.
- Gift Idea: Package the truffles in a decorative box or tin for a thoughtful homemade gift.

These Brazil Nut Chocolate Truffles are rich, decadent, and make for a delightful dessert or gift for chocolate lovers. Enjoy the combination of smooth chocolate and crunchy Brazil nuts in every bite!

Brazil Nut Soup

Ingredients:

- 1 cup Brazil nuts
- 1 tablespoon olive oil or butter
- 1 onion, finely chopped
- 2 cloves garlic, minced
- 2 carrots, diced
- 2 celery stalks, diced
- 1 potato, peeled and diced
- 4 cups vegetable or chicken broth
- 1 bay leaf
- 1/2 teaspoon ground cumin
- Salt and pepper, to taste
- Fresh parsley or cilantro, chopped (for garnish)
- Optional: 1/2 cup heavy cream or coconut cream for added richness

Instructions:

1. Prepare Brazil Nuts:
    - If using raw Brazil nuts, you can lightly toast them in a dry skillet over medium heat for a few minutes until fragrant. Let them cool, then chop or grind them finely in a food processor.
2. Sauté Vegetables:
    - In a large pot or Dutch oven, heat the olive oil or butter over medium heat. Add the chopped onion and sauté until translucent, about 5 minutes. Add the minced garlic and cook for another minute until fragrant.
3. Add Vegetables:
    - Stir in the diced carrots, celery, and potato. Cook for about 5 minutes, stirring occasionally, until the vegetables begin to soften.
4. Add Broth and Seasonings:
    - Pour in the vegetable or chicken broth. Add the bay leaf, ground cumin, salt, and pepper to taste. Bring the mixture to a boil, then reduce the heat to low. Cover and simmer for 20-25 minutes, or until the vegetables are tender.
5. Blend Soup:
    - Remove the bay leaf from the pot. Using an immersion blender or transfer the soup in batches to a blender, purée the soup until smooth and creamy.
6. Add Brazil Nuts and Cream (Optional):
    - Stir in the finely chopped or ground Brazil nuts. If using, add the heavy cream or coconut cream for added richness. Simmer for an additional 5-10 minutes to blend flavors.
7. Adjust Seasoning:
    - Taste the soup and adjust seasoning if needed, adding more salt, pepper, or cumin to taste.

- For best texture, chill the coated truffles in the refrigerator for another 30 minutes to set.
12. Serve:
    - Serve the Brazil Nut Chocolate Truffles at room temperature. Store any leftovers in an airtight container in the refrigerator for up to 1 week.

Tips:

- Variations: Experiment with different coatings such as melted chocolate for a double chocolate coating or crushed freeze-dried berries for a fruity twist.
- Gift Idea: Package the truffles in a decorative box or tin for a thoughtful homemade gift.

These Brazil Nut Chocolate Truffles are rich, decadent, and make for a delightful dessert or gift for chocolate lovers. Enjoy the combination of smooth chocolate and crunchy Brazil nuts in every bite!

Brazil Nut Soup

Ingredients:

- 1 cup Brazil nuts
- 1 tablespoon olive oil or butter
- 1 onion, finely chopped
- 2 cloves garlic, minced
- 2 carrots, diced
- 2 celery stalks, diced
- 1 potato, peeled and diced
- 4 cups vegetable or chicken broth
- 1 bay leaf
- 1/2 teaspoon ground cumin
- Salt and pepper, to taste
- Fresh parsley or cilantro, chopped (for garnish)
- Optional: 1/2 cup heavy cream or coconut cream for added richness

Instructions:

1. Prepare Brazil Nuts:
    - If using raw Brazil nuts, you can lightly toast them in a dry skillet over medium heat for a few minutes until fragrant. Let them cool, then chop or grind them finely in a food processor.
2. Sauté Vegetables:
    - In a large pot or Dutch oven, heat the olive oil or butter over medium heat. Add the chopped onion and sauté until translucent, about 5 minutes. Add the minced garlic and cook for another minute until fragrant.
3. Add Vegetables:
    - Stir in the diced carrots, celery, and potato. Cook for about 5 minutes, stirring occasionally, until the vegetables begin to soften.
4. Add Broth and Seasonings:
    - Pour in the vegetable or chicken broth. Add the bay leaf, ground cumin, salt, and pepper to taste. Bring the mixture to a boil, then reduce the heat to low. Cover and simmer for 20-25 minutes, or until the vegetables are tender.
5. Blend Soup:
    - Remove the bay leaf from the pot. Using an immersion blender or transfer the soup in batches to a blender, purée the soup until smooth and creamy.
6. Add Brazil Nuts and Cream (Optional):
    - Stir in the finely chopped or ground Brazil nuts. If using, add the heavy cream or coconut cream for added richness. Simmer for an additional 5-10 minutes to blend flavors.
7. Adjust Seasoning:
    - Taste the soup and adjust seasoning if needed, adding more salt, pepper, or cumin to taste.

8. Serve:
    - Ladle the Brazil Nut Soup into bowls. Garnish with chopped fresh parsley or cilantro, and optionally a drizzle of cream or a sprinkle of chopped Brazil nuts.

Tips:

- Texture: For a smoother soup, strain it through a fine mesh sieve after blending.
- Variations: Add other vegetables such as spinach, kale, or bell peppers for additional flavor and nutrition.
- Storage: Store leftover Brazil Nut Soup in an airtight container in the refrigerator for up to 3-4 days. Reheat gently on the stove before serving.

This Brazil Nut Soup is creamy, nutritious, and perfect for a comforting meal. It showcases the unique flavor of Brazil nuts while incorporating a variety of vegetables for a balanced and satisfying dish. Enjoy it warm with crusty bread for a complete meal experience!

Brazil Nut Stir Fry

Ingredients:

- 1 cup Brazil nuts, raw or lightly toasted
- 2 cups mixed vegetables (such as bell peppers, broccoli, snap peas, carrots, mushrooms)
- 2 tablespoons soy sauce (or tamari for gluten-free)
- 1 tablespoon oyster sauce (optional, for umami flavor)
- 1 tablespoon sesame oil
- 2 cloves garlic, minced
- 1-inch piece of ginger, grated
- 2 green onions, thinly sliced
- 1 tablespoon vegetable oil (for stir-frying)
- Cooked rice or noodles, for serving

Instructions:

1. Prepare Brazil Nuts:
    - If using raw Brazil nuts, you can lightly toast them in a dry skillet over medium heat for a few minutes until fragrant. Let them cool, then chop them into smaller pieces.
2. Prepare Vegetables:
    - Wash and chop the mixed vegetables into bite-sized pieces.
3. Make Stir Fry Sauce:
    - In a small bowl, whisk together soy sauce (or tamari), oyster sauce (if using), sesame oil, minced garlic, and grated ginger. Set aside.
4. Stir Fry:
    - Heat vegetable oil in a large skillet or wok over medium-high heat. Add the chopped Brazil nuts and stir fry for 2-3 minutes until lightly toasted and fragrant. Remove from the skillet and set aside.
5. Cook Vegetables:
    - In the same skillet or wok, add a bit more oil if needed. Add the mixed vegetables and stir fry for 5-6 minutes, or until they are tender-crisp and slightly charred.
6. Combine Ingredients:
    - Return the toasted Brazil nuts to the skillet with the vegetables. Pour the prepared stir fry sauce over the mixture.
7. Stir Fry Together:
    - Stir everything together well, ensuring the vegetables and nuts are coated evenly with the sauce. Cook for another 1-2 minutes until heated through.
8. Serve:
    - Serve the Brazil Nut Stir Fry hot over cooked rice or noodles. Garnish with sliced green onions for added freshness.

Tips:

- Variations: You can add protein such as tofu, chicken, shrimp, or beef to make it a complete meal.
- Spice: For a spicy kick, add crushed red pepper flakes or chopped fresh chili peppers.
- Storage: Store any leftover stir fry in an airtight container in the refrigerator for up to 3-4 days. Reheat gently on the stove or in the microwave before serving.

This Brazil Nut Stir Fry is quick to make and packed with flavors and textures. It's perfect for a weeknight dinner and allows you to enjoy the wholesome goodness of Brazil nuts along with fresh vegetables and savory seasonings.

Brazil Nut Smoothie

Ingredients:

- 1/4 cup Brazil nuts, raw or lightly toasted
- 1 ripe banana, peeled
- 1 cup spinach or kale leaves
- 1 tablespoon honey or maple syrup (optional, for sweetness)
- 1 cup almond milk or your preferred milk (adjust quantity for desired consistency)
- 1/2 teaspoon vanilla extract
- Ice cubes (optional)

Instructions:

1. Prepare Brazil Nuts:
   - If using raw Brazil nuts, you can lightly toast them in a dry skillet over medium heat for a few minutes until fragrant. Let them cool before using.
2. Blend Ingredients:
   - In a blender, combine the toasted Brazil nuts, ripe banana, spinach or kale leaves, honey or maple syrup (if using), almond milk, and vanilla extract.
3. Blend Until Smooth:
   - Blend on high speed until the mixture is smooth and creamy. If you prefer a colder smoothie, add a few ice cubes and blend again until well incorporated.
4. Adjust Consistency:
   - If the smoothie is too thick, add more almond milk or water, a little at a time, until you reach your desired consistency.
5. Serve:
   - Pour the Brazil Nut Smoothie into glasses. Optionally, garnish with a sprinkle of ground cinnamon or a few whole Brazil nuts on top.

Tips:

- Variations: You can customize your Brazil Nut Smoothie by adding other ingredients such as frozen berries, Greek yogurt for added creaminess, or a scoop of protein powder.
- Nutrition Boost: Brazil nuts are rich in selenium, which is beneficial for thyroid health and immune function.
- Storage: Enjoy the smoothie fresh for best taste and nutrition.

This Brazil Nut Smoothie recipe is a great way to start your day or as a satisfying snack. It's packed with nutrients, fiber, and natural sweetness from the banana, making it both delicious and nourishing. Adjust the ingredients to suit your taste preferences and dietary needs!

Brazil Nut Dipping Sauce

Ingredients:

- 1/2 cup Brazil nuts, raw or lightly toasted
- 1/4 cup water
- 2 tablespoons olive oil
- 2 tablespoons lemon juice
- 1 clove garlic, minced
- 1 teaspoon honey or maple syrup (optional, for sweetness)
- Salt and pepper, to taste
- Pinch of cayenne pepper or paprika (optional, for a hint of spice)

Instructions:

1. Prepare Brazil Nuts:
    - If using raw Brazil nuts, you can lightly toast them in a dry skillet over medium heat for a few minutes until fragrant. Let them cool before using.
2. Blend Ingredients:
    - In a food processor or blender, combine the toasted Brazil nuts, water, olive oil, lemon juice, minced garlic, and honey or maple syrup (if using).
3. Blend Until Smooth:
    - Process the mixture until smooth and creamy. You may need to scrape down the sides of the blender or food processor bowl occasionally to ensure even blending.
4. Season to Taste:
    - Add salt, pepper, and cayenne pepper or paprika (if using) to taste. Blend again briefly to incorporate the seasonings.
5. Adjust Consistency:
    - If the dipping sauce is too thick, you can thin it out with a little more water, 1 tablespoon at a time, until you reach your desired consistency.
6. Serve:
    - Transfer the Brazil Nut Dipping Sauce to a serving bowl. Optionally, garnish with a drizzle of olive oil and a sprinkle of paprika or chopped fresh herbs.

Tips:

- Variations: Experiment with adding fresh herbs like parsley or cilantro, or spices such as cumin or smoked paprika, to customize the flavor of your dipping sauce.
- Usage: Serve the Brazil Nut Dipping Sauce with raw vegetables, crackers, breadsticks, or use it as a sauce for grilled meats, seafood, or roasted vegetables.
- Storage: Store any leftover dipping sauce in an airtight container in the refrigerator for up to 3-4 days.

This Brazil Nut Dipping Sauce is creamy, nutty, and versatile, perfect for adding a unique twist to your snacks or meals. It's packed with flavor and healthy fats from Brazil nuts, making it a nutritious choice as well. Enjoy experimenting with different ingredients and serving ideas!

Brazil Nut Risotto

Ingredients:

- 1 cup Arborio rice
- 1/2 cup Brazil nuts, finely chopped
- 4 cups vegetable or chicken broth, kept warm
- 1 small onion, finely chopped
- 2 cloves garlic, minced
- 1/2 cup dry white wine (optional)
- 2 tablespoons olive oil or unsalted butter
- 1/2 cup grated Parmesan cheese (optional)
- Salt and pepper, to taste
- Fresh parsley or basil, chopped (for garnish)

Instructions:

1. Prepare Ingredients:
    - Finely chop the Brazil nuts. Keep the vegetable or chicken broth warm in a separate saucepan over low heat.
2. Sauté Onion and Garlic:
    - In a large skillet or saucepan, heat olive oil or butter over medium heat. Add the chopped onion and sauté until translucent, about 5 minutes. Add the minced garlic and cook for another minute until fragrant.
3. Toast Rice:
    - Add the Arborio rice to the skillet with the onion and garlic. Stir well to coat the rice with the oil or butter. Toast the rice for 1-2 minutes until it becomes slightly translucent around the edges.
4. Deglaze with Wine (Optional):
    - Pour in the white wine (if using) and stir constantly until the wine is absorbed by the rice.
5. Add Broth:
    - Begin adding the warm broth to the rice, one ladleful at a time, stirring continuously. Allow each addition of broth to be absorbed before adding more. This process helps release the starch from the rice, creating the creamy texture of risotto.
6. Cook Risotto:
    - Continue adding broth and stirring the rice for about 18-20 minutes, or until the rice is creamy and al dente (tender with a slight bite). You may not need to use all of the broth.
7. Incorporate Brazil Nuts:
    - In the last few minutes of cooking, stir in the finely chopped Brazil nuts. This adds a delicious nutty flavor and texture to the risotto.
8. Finish and Season:

- Remove the risotto from heat. Stir in grated Parmesan cheese (if using) until melted and well combined. Season with salt and pepper to taste.
9. Serve:
    - Serve the Brazil Nut Risotto immediately, garnished with chopped fresh parsley or basil. Optionally, sprinkle with additional grated Parmesan cheese before serving.

Tips:

- Variations: Add sautéed mushrooms, spinach, or roasted vegetables for added flavor and nutrition.
- Creaminess: For an extra creamy texture, stir in a tablespoon of mascarpone cheese or heavy cream at the end of cooking.
- Storage: Risotto is best enjoyed fresh but can be stored in an airtight container in the refrigerator for up to 2 days. Reheat gently on the stove with a splash of broth or water to loosen the rice.

This Brazil Nut Risotto recipe is a comforting and flavorful dish that showcases the unique taste of Brazil nuts. It's perfect for a special dinner or when you want to impress guests with a gourmet homemade meal. Enjoy the creamy goodness of risotto with the added crunch of Brazil nuts!

Brazil Nut Curry

Ingredients:

- 1 cup Brazil nuts, raw or lightly toasted
- 1 tablespoon vegetable oil or coconut oil
- 1 onion, finely chopped
- 3 cloves garlic, minced
- 1-inch piece of ginger, grated
- 1-2 tablespoons curry powder or curry paste (adjust to taste)
- 1 can (14 oz) coconut milk
- 1 cup vegetable broth or water
- 2 cups mixed vegetables (such as bell peppers, carrots, zucchini, peas)
- 1 can (14 oz) chickpeas, drained and rinsed
- Salt and pepper, to taste
- Fresh cilantro, chopped (for garnish)
- Cooked rice or naan bread, for serving

Instructions:

1. Prepare Brazil Nuts:
    - If using raw Brazil nuts, you can lightly toast them in a dry skillet over medium heat for a few minutes until fragrant. Let them cool, then chop them coarsely or grind them into a coarse meal in a food processor.
2. Sauté Onion, Garlic, and Ginger:
    - In a large pot or skillet, heat the vegetable oil or coconut oil over medium heat. Add the chopped onion and sauté until translucent, about 5 minutes. Add the minced garlic and grated ginger, and cook for another minute until fragrant.
3. Add Curry Powder/Paste:
    - Stir in the curry powder or curry paste and cook for 1-2 minutes, allowing the spices to bloom and become fragrant.
4. Add Coconut Milk and Broth:
    - Pour in the coconut milk and vegetable broth, stirring well to combine. Bring the mixture to a simmer.
5. Add Vegetables and Chickpeas:
    - Add the mixed vegetables and chickpeas to the pot. Simmer for 10-15 minutes, or until the vegetables are tender and cooked through.
6. Incorporate Brazil Nuts:
    - Stir in the coarsely chopped or ground Brazil nuts. Allow the curry to simmer for an additional 5 minutes, letting the flavors meld together. Season with salt and pepper to taste.
7. Serve:
    - Serve the Brazil Nut Curry hot, garnished with chopped fresh cilantro. Pair it with cooked rice or naan bread for a complete meal.

Tips:

- Protein: Add tofu, chicken, or shrimp for additional protein.
- Heat: Adjust the spiciness by adding more or less curry powder/paste or incorporating fresh chili peppers.
- Creaminess: For a creamier texture, blend a portion of the curry and then stir it back into the pot.

This Brazil Nut Curry is a rich, aromatic dish that's perfect for a comforting dinner. The Brazil nuts add a unique texture and flavor, making it a standout meal. Enjoy!

Brazil Nut Ice Cream

Ingredients:

- 1 cup Brazil nuts, raw or lightly toasted
- 1 tablespoon vegetable oil or coconut oil
- 1 onion, finely chopped
- 3 cloves garlic, minced
- 1-inch piece of ginger, grated
- 1-2 tablespoons curry powder or curry paste (adjust to taste)
- 1 can (14 oz) coconut milk
- 1 cup vegetable broth or water
- 2 cups mixed vegetables (such as bell peppers, carrots, zucchini, peas)
- 1 can (14 oz) chickpeas, drained and rinsed
- Salt and pepper, to taste
- Fresh cilantro, chopped (for garnish)
- Cooked rice or naan bread, for serving

Instructions:

1. Prepare Brazil Nuts:
    - If using raw Brazil nuts, you can lightly toast them in a dry skillet over medium heat for a few minutes until fragrant. Let them cool, then chop them coarsely or grind them into a coarse meal in a food processor.
2. Sauté Onion, Garlic, and Ginger:
    - In a large pot or skillet, heat the vegetable oil or coconut oil over medium heat. Add the chopped onion and sauté until translucent, about 5 minutes. Add the minced garlic and grated ginger, and cook for another minute until fragrant.
3. Add Curry Powder/Paste:
    - Stir in the curry powder or curry paste and cook for 1-2 minutes, allowing the spices to bloom and become fragrant.
4. Add Coconut Milk and Broth:
    - Pour in the coconut milk and vegetable broth, stirring well to combine. Bring the mixture to a simmer.
5. Add Vegetables and Chickpeas:
    - Add the mixed vegetables and chickpeas to the pot. Simmer for 10-15 minutes, or until the vegetables are tender and cooked through.
6. Incorporate Brazil Nuts:
    - Stir in the coarsely chopped or ground Brazil nuts. Allow the curry to simmer for an additional 5 minutes, letting the flavors meld together. Season with salt and pepper to taste.
7. Serve:
    - Serve the Brazil Nut Curry hot, garnished with chopped fresh cilantro. Pair it with cooked rice or naan bread for a complete meal.

Tips:

- Protein: Add tofu, chicken, or shrimp for additional protein.
- Heat: Adjust the spiciness by adding more or less curry powder/paste or incorporating fresh chili peppers.
- Creaminess: For a creamier texture, blend a portion of the curry and then stir it back into the pot.

This Brazil Nut Curry is a rich, aromatic dish that's perfect for a comforting dinner. The Brazil nuts add a unique texture and flavor, making it a standout meal. Enjoy!

Brazil Nut Salsa

Ingredients:

- 1/2 cup Brazil nuts, raw or lightly toasted
- 3 medium tomatoes, finely diced
- 1 small red onion, finely chopped
- 1 jalapeño pepper, seeded and finely chopped (optional, for heat)
- 1/4 cup fresh cilantro, chopped
- 1 clove garlic, minced
- 1/4 cup lime juice (about 2 limes)
- 1 tablespoon olive oil
- Salt and pepper, to taste

Instructions:

1. Prepare Brazil Nuts:
    - If using raw Brazil nuts, you can lightly toast them in a dry skillet over medium heat for a few minutes until fragrant. Let them cool, then chop them finely.
2. Combine Fresh Ingredients:
    - In a medium bowl, combine the diced tomatoes, chopped red onion, jalapeño pepper (if using), chopped cilantro, and minced garlic.
3. Add Brazil Nuts:
    - Stir in the finely chopped Brazil nuts.
4. Dress the Salsa:
    - Add the lime juice and olive oil to the mixture. Toss everything together until well combined.
5. Season:
    - Season the salsa with salt and pepper to taste. Adjust the lime juice and olive oil if needed.
6. Serve:
    - Serve the Brazil Nut Salsa immediately with tortilla chips, as a topping for grilled meats, or as a fresh accompaniment to your favorite dishes.

Tips:

- Storage: Store any leftover salsa in an airtight container in the refrigerator for up to 2 days. The flavors will meld together over time, but it's best enjoyed fresh.
- Variations: Add diced avocado for a creamier texture, or include other fruits like mango or pineapple for a sweet and savory twist.
- Heat: Adjust the amount of jalapeño or add a different type of chili pepper to control the heat level.

This Brazil Nut Salsa is a fresh, crunchy, and flavorful addition to any meal. It's perfect for summer gatherings, barbecues, or simply as a nutritious snack. Enjoy the unique twist that Brazil nuts bring to this classic dish!

Brazil Nut Tapenade

Ingredients:

- 1/2 cup Brazil nuts, raw or lightly toasted
- 3 medium tomatoes, finely diced
- 1 small red onion, finely chopped
- 1 jalapeño pepper, seeded and finely chopped (optional, for heat)
- 1/4 cup fresh cilantro, chopped
- 1 clove garlic, minced
- 1/4 cup lime juice (about 2 limes)
- 1 tablespoon olive oil
- Salt and pepper, to taste

Instructions:

1. Prepare Brazil Nuts:
   - If using raw Brazil nuts, you can lightly toast them in a dry skillet over medium heat for a few minutes until fragrant. Let them cool, then chop them finely.
2. Combine Fresh Ingredients:
   - In a medium bowl, combine the diced tomatoes, chopped red onion, jalapeño pepper (if using), chopped cilantro, and minced garlic.
3. Add Brazil Nuts:
   - Stir in the finely chopped Brazil nuts.
4. Dress the Salsa:
   - Add the lime juice and olive oil to the mixture. Toss everything together until well combined.
5. Season:
   - Season the salsa with salt and pepper to taste. Adjust the lime juice and olive oil if needed.
6. Serve:
   - Serve the Brazil Nut Salsa immediately with tortilla chips, as a topping for grilled meats, or as a fresh accompaniment to your favorite dishes.

Tips:

- Storage: Store any leftover salsa in an airtight container in the refrigerator for up to 2 days. The flavors will meld together over time, but it's best enjoyed fresh.
- Variations: Add diced avocado for a creamier texture, or include other fruits like mango or pineapple for a sweet and savory twist.
- Heat: Adjust the amount of jalapeño or add a different type of chili pepper to control the heat level.

This Brazil Nut Salsa is a fresh, crunchy, and flavorful addition to any meal. It's perfect for summer gatherings, barbecues, or simply as a nutritious snack. Enjoy the unique twist that Brazil nuts bring to this classic dish!

Brazil Nut Tapenade

Ingredients:

- 1/2 cup Brazil nuts, raw or lightly toasted
- 1 cup pitted black olives (such as Kalamata)
- 1 cup pitted green olives (such as Castelvetrano)
- 2 tablespoons capers, drained
- 2 cloves garlic, minced
- 1 tablespoon lemon juice
- 3 tablespoons olive oil
- 1/4 cup fresh parsley, chopped
- Salt and pepper, to taste

Instructions:

1. Prepare Brazil Nuts:
    - If using raw Brazil nuts, you can lightly toast them in a dry skillet over medium heat for a few minutes until fragrant. Let them cool, then chop them coarsely.
2. Combine Ingredients:
    - In a food processor, combine the chopped Brazil nuts, black olives, green olives, capers, minced garlic, lemon juice, and olive oil.
3. Pulse to Desired Consistency:
    - Pulse the mixture until it reaches your desired consistency. For a chunkier tapenade, pulse a few times, and for a smoother spread, process it longer. Scrape down the sides of the bowl as needed.
4. Add Parsley and Season:
    - Add the chopped fresh parsley to the food processor and pulse a few more times to incorporate. Season with salt and pepper to taste.
5. Serve:
    - Transfer the Brazil Nut Tapenade to a serving bowl. Serve it with crusty bread, crackers, or as a spread for sandwiches and wraps.

Tips:

- Storage: Store any leftover tapenade in an airtight container in the refrigerator for up to 5 days. The flavors will meld together over time, making it even more delicious.
- Variations: Experiment with additional ingredients like sun-dried tomatoes, roasted red peppers, or fresh herbs like basil or thyme for different flavor profiles.
- Uses: Besides being a great spread for bread and crackers, tapenade can also be used as a topping for grilled chicken, fish, or vegetables.

This Brazil Nut Tapenade is a versatile and flavorful spread that adds a gourmet touch to any dish. Enjoy the unique combination of Brazil nuts and olives for a delightful appetizer or condiment.

Brazil Nut Croquettes

Ingredients:

- 1 cup Brazil nuts, finely chopped
- 1 cup mashed potatoes (about 2 medium potatoes)
- 1/2 cup grated cheese (such as Parmesan or cheddar)
- 1 small onion, finely chopped
- 2 cloves garlic, minced
- 1 tablespoon fresh parsley, chopped
- 1 egg, lightly beaten
- Salt and pepper, to taste
- 1 cup breadcrumbs
- Oil for frying (vegetable, canola, or sunflower oil works well)

Instructions:

1. Prepare Brazil Nuts:
    - If using raw Brazil nuts, you can lightly toast them in a dry skillet over medium heat for a few minutes until fragrant. Let them cool, then finely chop or process them into small pieces in a food processor.
2. Prepare Potatoes:
    - Peel and boil the potatoes until tender. Mash them until smooth and let them cool slightly.
3. Combine Ingredients:
    - In a large bowl, combine the mashed potatoes, finely chopped Brazil nuts, grated cheese, chopped onion, minced garlic, chopped parsley, and beaten egg. Mix well until all ingredients are evenly incorporated. Season with salt and pepper to taste.
4. Form Croquettes:
    - Shape the mixture into small, cylindrical or oval croquettes (about 2 inches long). If the mixture is too sticky, you can dampen your hands with water to help shape the croquettes.
5. Coat with Breadcrumbs:
    - Roll each croquette in breadcrumbs until fully coated. Place them on a baking sheet or plate.
6. Heat Oil:
    - Heat about 1 inch of oil in a large skillet or frying pan over medium heat until it reaches 350°F (175°C). You can test the oil by dropping a small piece of bread into it; it should sizzle and turn golden brown in about 1 minute.
7. Fry Croquettes:
    - Fry the croquettes in batches, making sure not to overcrowd the pan. Cook each croquette for about 2-3 minutes per side, or until golden brown and crispy. Use a slotted spoon to transfer the cooked croquettes to a paper towel-lined plate to drain any excess oil.

8. Serve:
   - Serve the Brazil Nut Croquettes hot, garnished with additional chopped parsley if desired. They pair well with a dipping sauce like aioli, spicy mayo, or a simple yogurt dip.

Tips:

- Baking Option: For a healthier alternative, you can bake the croquettes. Preheat the oven to 400°F (200°C), place the croquettes on a baking sheet lined with parchment paper, and lightly spray them with cooking oil. Bake for 20-25 minutes, turning halfway through, until golden and crispy.
- Variations: Add other ingredients like finely chopped cooked spinach, grated carrots, or corn kernels for added flavor and texture.
- Storage: Store any leftover croquettes in an airtight container in the refrigerator for up to 3 days. Reheat in the oven or air fryer to maintain their crispiness.

Enjoy these Brazil Nut Croquettes as a delightful and crunchy treat that's sure to impress your family and friends!

Brazil Nut Cheesecake

Ingredients:

For the crust:

- 1 cup Brazil nuts, finely ground
- 1 cup graham cracker crumbs
- 1/4 cup granulated sugar
- 1/2 cup unsalted butter, melted

For the filling:

- 3 packages (8 oz each) cream cheese, softened
- 1 cup granulated sugar
- 3 large eggs
- 1 teaspoon vanilla extract
- 1/2 cup sour cream
- 1/2 cup finely chopped Brazil nuts

For the topping (optional):

- 1 cup sour cream
- 2 tablespoons powdered sugar
- 1 teaspoon vanilla extract
- Additional chopped Brazil nuts for garnish

Instructions:

1. Preheat Oven:
    - Preheat your oven to 350°F (175°C). Grease a 9-inch springform pan.
2. Prepare the Crust:
    - In a medium bowl, combine the ground Brazil nuts, graham cracker crumbs, granulated sugar, and melted butter. Mix until the crumbs are evenly coated with butter.
    - Press the mixture firmly into the bottom of the prepared springform pan to form an even crust.
    - Bake the crust for 10 minutes, then remove it from the oven and let it cool while you prepare the filling.
3. Prepare the Filling:
    - In a large bowl, beat the softened cream cheese with an electric mixer until smooth and creamy.
    - Gradually add the granulated sugar, beating until well combined.
    - Add the eggs one at a time, beating well after each addition.
    - Mix in the vanilla extract and sour cream until smooth.
    - Gently fold in the finely chopped Brazil nuts.

4. Bake the Cheesecake:
    - Pour the filling over the cooled crust, spreading it evenly.
    - Bake the cheesecake in the preheated oven for 50-60 minutes, or until the center is set but still slightly jiggly.
    - Turn off the oven and let the cheesecake cool in the oven with the door slightly ajar for about an hour. This helps prevent cracking.
5. Prepare the Topping (Optional):
    - In a small bowl, combine the sour cream, powdered sugar, and vanilla extract.
    - Spread the mixture evenly over the top of the cooled cheesecake.
    - Sprinkle additional chopped Brazil nuts on top for garnish.
6. Chill the Cheesecake:
    - Refrigerate the cheesecake for at least 4 hours, or overnight, before serving. This allows the flavors to meld and the cheesecake to set properly.
7. Serve:
    - Remove the cheesecake from the springform pan and transfer it to a serving plate.
    - Slice and serve chilled. Enjoy your creamy and nutty Brazil Nut Cheesecake!

Tips:

- Crust Alternatives: You can substitute graham cracker crumbs with other cookie crumbs like digestive biscuits or vanilla wafers.
- Nut Substitution: If you don't have enough Brazil nuts, you can mix in other nuts like almonds or pecans for a varied flavor.
- Storage: Store any leftover cheesecake in an airtight container in the refrigerator for up to 5 days. Cheesecake can also be frozen for up to 2 months.

This Brazil Nut Cheesecake is a decadent dessert that combines the creamy texture of classic cheesecake with the unique flavor of Brazil nuts, making it a standout treat for any occasion.

Brazil Nut Torte

Ingredients:

For the crust:

- 1 cup Brazil nuts, finely ground
- 1 cup graham cracker crumbs
- 1/4 cup granulated sugar
- 1/2 cup unsalted butter, melted

For the filling:

- 3 packages (8 oz each) cream cheese, softened
- 1 cup granulated sugar
- 3 large eggs
- 1 teaspoon vanilla extract
- 1/2 cup sour cream
- 1/2 cup finely chopped Brazil nuts

For the topping (optional):

- 1 cup sour cream
- 2 tablespoons powdered sugar
- 1 teaspoon vanilla extract
- Additional chopped Brazil nuts for garnish

Instructions:

1. Preheat Oven:
    - Preheat your oven to 350°F (175°C). Grease a 9-inch springform pan.
2. Prepare the Crust:
    - In a medium bowl, combine the ground Brazil nuts, graham cracker crumbs, granulated sugar, and melted butter. Mix until the crumbs are evenly coated with butter.
    - Press the mixture firmly into the bottom of the prepared springform pan to form an even crust.
    - Bake the crust for 10 minutes, then remove it from the oven and let it cool while you prepare the filling.
3. Prepare the Filling:
    - In a large bowl, beat the softened cream cheese with an electric mixer until smooth and creamy.
    - Gradually add the granulated sugar, beating until well combined.
    - Add the eggs one at a time, beating well after each addition.
    - Mix in the vanilla extract and sour cream until smooth.
    - Gently fold in the finely chopped Brazil nuts.

4. **Bake the Cheesecake:**
   - Pour the filling over the cooled crust, spreading it evenly.
   - Bake the cheesecake in the preheated oven for 50-60 minutes, or until the center is set but still slightly jiggly.
   - Turn off the oven and let the cheesecake cool in the oven with the door slightly ajar for about an hour. This helps prevent cracking.
5. **Prepare the Topping (Optional):**
   - In a small bowl, combine the sour cream, powdered sugar, and vanilla extract.
   - Spread the mixture evenly over the top of the cooled cheesecake.
   - Sprinkle additional chopped Brazil nuts on top for garnish.
6. **Chill the Cheesecake:**
   - Refrigerate the cheesecake for at least 4 hours, or overnight, before serving. This allows the flavors to meld and the cheesecake to set properly.
7. **Serve:**
   - Remove the cheesecake from the springform pan and transfer it to a serving plate.
   - Slice and serve chilled. Enjoy your creamy and nutty Brazil Nut Cheesecake!

Tips:

- Crust Alternatives: You can substitute graham cracker crumbs with other cookie crumbs like digestive biscuits or vanilla wafers.
- Nut Substitution: If you don't have enough Brazil nuts, you can mix in other nuts like almonds or pecans for a varied flavor.
- Storage: Store any leftover cheesecake in an airtight container in the refrigerator for up to 5 days. Cheesecake can also be frozen for up to 2 months.

This Brazil Nut Cheesecake is a decadent dessert that combines the creamy texture of classic cheesecake with the unique flavor of Brazil nuts, making it a standout treat for any occasion.

Brazil Nut Torte

Ingredients:

For the torte:

- 1 1/2 cups Brazil nuts, finely ground
- 1 cup all-purpose flour
- 1 teaspoon baking powder
- 1/2 teaspoon salt
- 1/2 cup unsalted butter, softened
- 1 cup granulated sugar
- 3 large eggs
- 1 teaspoon vanilla extract
- 1/2 cup milk

For the glaze:

- 1/2 cup dark chocolate, chopped
- 1/4 cup heavy cream
- 1 tablespoon unsalted butter

For garnish (optional):

- Chopped Brazil nuts
- Whipped cream or vanilla ice cream

Instructions:

1. Preheat Oven:
    - Preheat your oven to 350°F (175°C). Grease and flour an 8-inch round cake pan, or line it with parchment paper.
2. Prepare Dry Ingredients:
    - In a medium bowl, combine the finely ground Brazil nuts, all-purpose flour, baking powder, and salt. Mix well and set aside.
3. Cream Butter and Sugar:
    - In a large bowl, beat the softened butter and granulated sugar with an electric mixer until light and fluffy, about 3-5 minutes.
4. Add Eggs and Vanilla:
    - Add the eggs one at a time, beating well after each addition. Mix in the vanilla extract.
5. Combine Wet and Dry Ingredients:
    - Gradually add the dry ingredients to the butter mixture, alternating with the milk, beginning and ending with the dry ingredients. Mix until just combined.
6. Bake the Torte:
    - Pour the batter into the prepared cake pan and smooth the top with a spatula.

- Bake in the preheated oven for 30-35 minutes, or until a toothpick inserted into the center of the torte comes out clean.
- Allow the torte to cool in the pan for 10 minutes, then transfer it to a wire rack to cool completely.

7. Prepare the Chocolate Glaze:
   - In a small saucepan, heat the heavy cream over medium heat until it begins to simmer. Remove from heat and add the chopped dark chocolate and unsalted butter. Let it sit for a minute, then stir until smooth and glossy.
8. Glaze the Torte:
   - Once the torte has cooled completely, pour the chocolate glaze over the top, letting it drip down the sides. Use a spatula to spread the glaze evenly if needed.
9. Garnish and Serve:
   - Optionally, garnish the torte with additional chopped Brazil nuts. Serve with whipped cream or vanilla ice cream if desired.

Tips:

- Storage: Store any leftover torte in an airtight container at room temperature for up to 3 days or in the refrigerator for up to a week. Allow it to come to room temperature before serving.
- Nut Grinding: For a finer texture, grind the Brazil nuts in a food processor until they resemble coarse flour, but be careful not to over-process and turn them into nut butter.
- Flavor Variations: Add a hint of orange zest or a splash of coffee liqueur to the batter for additional flavor complexity.

This Brazil Nut Torte is a decadent and elegant dessert that's sure to impress. The combination of rich, nutty flavor and smooth chocolate glaze makes it a delightful treat for any occasion. Enjoy!

Brazil Nut Fudge

Ingredients:

- 2 cups granulated sugar
- 3/4 cup unsalted butter
- 2/3 cup evaporated milk
- 2 cups semisweet chocolate chips
- 1 jar (7 oz) marshmallow creme
- 1 cup chopped Brazil nuts
- 1 teaspoon vanilla extract
- 1/4 teaspoon salt

Instructions:

1. Prepare the Pan:
    - Line an 8-inch square baking pan with aluminum foil, extending the foil over the edges. Grease the foil with butter or non-stick spray.
2. Combine Sugar, Butter, and Milk:
    - In a medium saucepan, combine the granulated sugar, unsalted butter, and evaporated milk. Bring the mixture to a boil over medium heat, stirring constantly.
3. Boil the Mixture:
    - Once the mixture reaches a rolling boil, continue to cook and stir for 4-5 minutes. Use a candy thermometer to ensure the mixture reaches 234°F (112°C), the soft-ball stage.
4. Add Chocolate Chips and Marshmallow Creme:
    - Remove the saucepan from heat. Stir in the semisweet chocolate chips until melted and smooth. Add the marshmallow creme, vanilla extract, and salt, and stir until well combined.
5. Add Brazil Nuts:
    - Fold in the chopped Brazil nuts until evenly distributed throughout the fudge mixture.
6. Pour into Prepared Pan:
    - Pour the fudge mixture into the prepared baking pan. Use a spatula to spread it evenly and smooth the top.
7. Cool and Set:
    - Let the fudge cool to room temperature, then refrigerate for at least 2 hours, or until firm.
8. Cut and Serve:
    - Once the fudge is set, use the foil overhang to lift it out of the pan. Place it on a cutting board and cut it into small squares.

Tips:

- Storage: Store the fudge in an airtight container at room temperature for up to 2 weeks or in the refrigerator for up to a month. For longer storage, you can freeze the fudge for up to 3 months.
- Variations: Add a swirl of caramel or peanut butter to the fudge mixture before it sets for a different flavor profile. You can also add other nuts or dried fruits if you like.
- Presentation: For an extra touch, sprinkle a few chopped Brazil nuts on top of the fudge before it sets to give it a more appealing look.

Enjoy this Brazil Nut Fudge as a delightful, nutty treat that's perfect for special occasions, gift-giving, or simply indulging in a sweet, homemade dessert.

Brazil Nut Pudding

Ingredients:

- 1 cup Brazil nuts, finely ground
- 2 cups whole milk
- 1/2 cup heavy cream
- 1/2 cup granulated sugar
- 3 tablespoons cornstarch
- 1/4 teaspoon salt
- 3 large egg yolks
- 2 teaspoons vanilla extract

Instructions:

1. Prepare Brazil Nuts:
    - Finely grind the Brazil nuts using a food processor or blender until they reach a flour-like consistency.
2. Heat Milk and Cream:
    - In a medium saucepan, combine the whole milk and heavy cream. Heat over medium heat until the mixture is hot but not boiling.
3. Mix Dry Ingredients:
    - In a separate bowl, whisk together the granulated sugar, cornstarch, and salt.
4. Temper the Egg Yolks:
    - In another bowl, lightly beat the egg yolks. Gradually add a small amount of the hot milk mixture to the egg yolks, whisking constantly to prevent the yolks from curdling.
5. Combine Ingredients:
    - Slowly whisk the egg yolk mixture back into the saucepan with the remaining hot milk and cream. Add the ground Brazil nuts to the mixture.
6. Cook the Pudding:
    - Cook the mixture over medium heat, stirring constantly, until it thickens and begins to bubble. This should take about 5-7 minutes. Once it reaches the desired thickness, remove the saucepan from the heat.
7. Add Vanilla Extract:
    - Stir in the vanilla extract.
8. Strain the Pudding:
    - For a smoother texture, strain the pudding through a fine-mesh sieve into a bowl to remove any lumps or larger pieces of nuts.
9. Chill the Pudding:
    - Cover the surface of the pudding with plastic wrap to prevent a skin from forming. Let it cool to room temperature, then refrigerate for at least 2 hours, or until well chilled.
10. Serve:

- Once the pudding is chilled, give it a good stir before serving. Spoon the pudding into individual serving dishes and garnish with additional chopped Brazil nuts if desired.

Tips:

- Storage: Store any leftover pudding in an airtight container in the refrigerator for up to 3 days.
- Variations: For added flavor, you can incorporate a teaspoon of cinnamon or a tablespoon of cocoa powder into the dry ingredients. You can also fold in whipped cream before serving for an extra creamy texture.
- Serving Suggestions: This pudding pairs wonderfully with fresh fruit, a dollop of whipped cream, or a drizzle of caramel sauce.

Enjoy this creamy, nutty Brazil Nut Pudding as a delightful and unique dessert that's perfect for any occasion!

Brazil Nut Stuffed Mushrooms

Ingredients:

- 20 large white or cremini mushrooms
- 1 cup Brazil nuts, finely chopped
- 2 tablespoons olive oil
- 1 small onion, finely chopped
- 2 cloves garlic, minced
- 1/2 cup breadcrumbs
- 1/4 cup grated Parmesan cheese
- 2 tablespoons fresh parsley, chopped
- 1 teaspoon dried thyme
- Salt and pepper, to taste
- 1/4 cup cream cheese, softened
- 2 tablespoons unsalted butter, melted

Instructions:

1. Preheat Oven:
    - Preheat your oven to 375°F (190°C). Line a baking sheet with parchment paper or lightly grease it.
2. Prepare the Mushrooms:
    - Clean the mushrooms with a damp paper towel. Remove the stems and set them aside. Hollow out the mushroom caps slightly to create more space for the filling, if necessary.
3. Chop Mushroom Stems:
    - Finely chop the mushroom stems.
4. Cook the Filling:
    - Heat the olive oil in a skillet over medium heat. Add the chopped onion and cook until softened, about 3-4 minutes.
    - Add the chopped mushroom stems and minced garlic to the skillet. Cook for another 3-4 minutes, until the mushroom stems are tender and any liquid has evaporated.
    - Stir in the finely chopped Brazil nuts, breadcrumbs, Parmesan cheese, fresh parsley, dried thyme, salt, and pepper. Cook for another 2-3 minutes until the mixture is well combined and heated through.
    - Remove the skillet from heat and stir in the softened cream cheese until the mixture is well combined.
5. Stuff the Mushrooms:
    - Spoon the filling into each mushroom cap, pressing it down slightly to ensure it is well packed.
6. Prepare for Baking:
    - Arrange the stuffed mushrooms on the prepared baking sheet. Brush the tops with melted butter.

7. Bake:
   - Bake in the preheated oven for 20-25 minutes, or until the mushrooms are tender and the tops are golden brown.
8. Serve:
   - Remove the stuffed mushrooms from the oven and let them cool slightly before serving.

Tips:

- Variations: You can add other ingredients to the filling, such as chopped spinach, sun-dried tomatoes, or different herbs like basil or oregano for extra flavor.
- Cheese Options: Substitute the Parmesan with other cheeses like Gruyere, feta, or mozzarella for a different taste profile.
- Storage: Store any leftover stuffed mushrooms in an airtight container in the refrigerator for up to 3 days. Reheat in the oven or microwave before serving.

These Brazil Nut Stuffed Mushrooms are sure to be a hit with their rich, nutty flavor and savory filling. Enjoy them as a tasty appetizer or a side dish!

Brazil Nut Biscotti

Ingredients:

- 1 cup Brazil nuts, coarsely chopped
- 2 cups all-purpose flour
- 1 cup granulated sugar
- 1 teaspoon baking powder
- 1/4 teaspoon salt
- 3 large eggs
- 1 teaspoon vanilla extract
- 1 teaspoon almond extract
- 1/2 teaspoon ground cinnamon (optional)

Instructions:

1. Preheat Oven:
    - Preheat your oven to 350°F (175°C). Line a baking sheet with parchment paper.
2. Mix Dry Ingredients:
    - In a large bowl, whisk together the flour, sugar, baking powder, salt, and ground cinnamon (if using).
3. Beat Eggs and Extracts:
    - In a separate bowl, beat the eggs, vanilla extract, and almond extract until well combined.
4. Combine Wet and Dry Ingredients:
    - Add the wet ingredients to the dry ingredients and mix until a dough forms. It will be sticky.
    - Fold in the chopped Brazil nuts until evenly distributed.
5. Shape the Dough:
    - On a lightly floured surface, divide the dough in half. Shape each half into a log about 12 inches long and 2 inches wide.
    - Place the logs on the prepared baking sheet, spacing them apart.
6. First Bake:
    - Bake in the preheated oven for 25-30 minutes, or until the logs are golden brown and firm to the touch.
    - Remove from the oven and let the logs cool on the baking sheet for about 10 minutes.
7. Slice and Second Bake:
    - Reduce the oven temperature to 325°F (165°C).
    - Transfer the cooled logs to a cutting board. Using a serrated knife, cut the logs diagonally into 1/2-inch thick slices.
    - Place the slices cut side down on the baking sheet.
    - Bake for an additional 10-15 minutes, or until the biscotti are golden and crisp. Flip the slices halfway through the baking time for even crispness.
8. Cool and Serve:

- Remove the biscotti from the oven and let them cool completely on a wire rack.

Tips:

- Storage: Store the biscotti in an airtight container at room temperature for up to two weeks. They can also be frozen for up to three months.
- Variations: Add 1/2 cup of chocolate chips or dried fruit (such as cranberries or apricots) to the dough for extra flavor and texture.
- Dipping: For an extra treat, dip one end of the cooled biscotti in melted chocolate and let it set before serving.

Enjoy your Brazil Nut Biscotti with a cup of coffee, tea, or hot chocolate for a delightful and satisfying treat!

Brazil Nut Quiche

Ingredients:

For the crust:

- 1 1/4 cups all-purpose flour
- 1/2 teaspoon salt
- 1/2 cup unsalted butter, cold and cubed
- 3-4 tablespoons ice water

For the filling:

- 1 cup Brazil nuts, chopped
- 1 tablespoon olive oil
- 1 small onion, finely chopped
- 1 clove garlic, minced
- 1 cup spinach, chopped (optional)
- 4 large eggs
- 1 cup heavy cream or half-and-half
- 1/2 cup shredded cheese (such as Swiss, Gruyere, or cheddar)
- Salt and pepper, to taste
- Pinch of nutmeg (optional)
- Fresh parsley or chives, chopped for garnish

Instructions:

1. Prepare the Crust:
   - In a food processor, combine the flour and salt. Add the cold cubed butter and pulse until the mixture resembles coarse crumbs.
   - Gradually add the ice water, 1 tablespoon at a time, pulsing until the dough comes together. You may not need to use all the water.
   - Transfer the dough to a lightly floured surface and shape it into a disk. Wrap in plastic wrap and refrigerate for at least 30 minutes.
2. Preheat Oven:
   - Preheat your oven to 375°F (190°C).
3. Roll Out and Line the Pie Dish:
   - On a lightly floured surface, roll out the chilled dough into a circle about 12 inches in diameter. Carefully transfer the dough to a 9-inch pie dish. Trim any excess dough and crimp the edges as desired.
4. Blind Bake the Crust (optional):
   - Line the pie crust with parchment paper and fill with pie weights or dried beans. Bake for 15 minutes. Remove the parchment paper and weights, then bake for an additional 5 minutes until the crust is just set and lightly golden. Remove from the oven and set aside.

5. Prepare the Filling:
    - In a skillet, heat the olive oil over medium heat. Add the chopped Brazil nuts and toast for 2-3 minutes until lightly browned and fragrant. Remove from the skillet and set aside.
    - In the same skillet, add the chopped onion and cook until softened, about 3-4 minutes. Add the minced garlic and cook for another 1 minute. Stir in the chopped spinach (if using) and cook until wilted. Remove from heat and let cool slightly.
6. Assemble the Quiche:
    - In a bowl, whisk together the eggs and heavy cream until well combined. Season with salt, pepper, and a pinch of nutmeg if desired.
    - Stir in the shredded cheese, toasted Brazil nuts, and cooked onion mixture.
    - Pour the filling into the partially baked pie crust, spreading it out evenly.
7. Bake the Quiche:
    - Place the quiche in the preheated oven and bake for 35-40 minutes, or until the filling is set and the top is golden brown.
8. Cool and Serve:
    - Remove the quiche from the oven and let it cool for 10 minutes before slicing.
    - Garnish with chopped fresh parsley or chives before serving.

Tips:

- Variations: You can add other vegetables like mushrooms or bell peppers to the filling for added flavor and texture.
- Make Ahead: You can prepare the crust and filling ahead of time and assemble and bake the quiche just before serving.
- Storage: Leftover quiche can be stored in the refrigerator for up to 3 days. Reheat slices in the oven or microwave before serving.

This Brazil Nut Quiche is a flavorful and satisfying dish that can be enjoyed for brunch, lunch, or dinner. It's versatile and sure to be a hit with family and friends!

Brazil Nut Stuffed Peppers

Ingredients:

- 4 large bell peppers (any color), tops cut off and seeds removed
- 1 cup cooked quinoa or rice
- 1 cup Brazil nuts, finely chopped
- 1 tablespoon olive oil
- 1 small onion, finely chopped
- 2 cloves garlic, minced
- 1/2 cup diced tomatoes (canned or fresh)
- 1/2 cup corn kernels (canned or frozen)
- 1/2 cup black beans, drained and rinsed
- 1 teaspoon ground cumin
- 1/2 teaspoon smoked paprika
- Salt and pepper, to taste
- 1/2 cup shredded cheese (such as cheddar or mozzarella), optional
- Fresh cilantro or parsley, chopped, for garnish

Instructions:

1. Preheat Oven:
     - Preheat your oven to 375°F (190°C). Lightly grease a baking dish that can hold the stuffed peppers upright.
2. Prepare the Peppers:
     - Cut the tops off the bell peppers and remove the seeds and membranes. If needed, trim the bottoms slightly to help them stand upright in the baking dish.
3. Prepare the Filling:
     - In a large skillet, heat olive oil over medium heat. Add the chopped onion and cook until softened, about 3-4 minutes.
     - Add the minced garlic and cook for another 1 minute until fragrant.
     - Stir in the diced tomatoes, corn kernels, black beans, ground cumin, smoked paprika, salt, and pepper. Cook for 2-3 minutes until heated through.
     - Remove the skillet from heat and stir in the cooked quinoa (or rice) and finely chopped Brazil nuts. Adjust seasoning to taste.
4. Stuff the Peppers:
     - Spoon the filling mixture into each bell pepper until they are generously filled. Press down gently to pack the filling.
5. Bake the Stuffed Peppers:
     - Place the stuffed peppers upright in the prepared baking dish. If desired, sprinkle shredded cheese over the tops of the stuffed peppers.
     - Cover the baking dish with foil and bake in the preheated oven for 30-35 minutes, or until the peppers are tender and the filling is heated through.
     - Remove the foil during the last 10 minutes of baking to allow the cheese to melt and brown slightly.

6. Serve:
    - Remove the stuffed peppers from the oven and let them cool for a few minutes before serving.
    - Garnish with chopped fresh cilantro or parsley before serving.

Tips:

- Variations: You can add diced cooked chicken, ground beef, or tofu to the filling mixture for added protein.
- Make Ahead: You can prepare the filling ahead of time and store it in the refrigerator. Stuff the peppers and bake them just before serving.
- Storage: Leftover stuffed peppers can be stored in an airtight container in the refrigerator for up to 3 days. Reheat in the oven or microwave before serving.

These Brazil Nut Stuffed Peppers are a nutritious and satisfying meal that's perfect for a vegetarian main course or a flavorful side dish. Enjoy the combination of textures and flavors in every bite!

Brazil Nut Chutney

Ingredients:

- 1 cup Brazil nuts, finely chopped
- 1 tablespoon olive oil
- 1 small onion, finely chopped
- 2 cloves garlic, minced
- 1-inch piece of ginger, peeled and minced
- 1/2 teaspoon cumin seeds
- 1/4 teaspoon ground coriander
- 1/4 teaspoon ground turmeric
- 1/4 teaspoon cayenne pepper (adjust to taste)
- 1/2 cup apple cider vinegar
- 1/4 cup brown sugar (adjust to taste)
- 1/2 cup raisins or chopped dried apricots
- Salt, to taste
- Water, as needed

Instructions:

1. Prepare Brazil Nuts:
    - Finely chop the Brazil nuts using a food processor or a sharp knife.
2. Cooking the Chutney:
    - Heat the olive oil in a saucepan over medium heat. Add the chopped onion and cook until softened, about 3-4 minutes.
    - Add the minced garlic, ginger, cumin seeds, ground coriander, ground turmeric, and cayenne pepper. Cook for another 1-2 minutes until fragrant.
3. Add Vinegar and Sugar:
    - Pour in the apple cider vinegar and brown sugar. Stir well to combine and bring the mixture to a simmer.
4. Simmer the Chutney:
    - Add the chopped Brazil nuts and raisins (or dried apricots) to the saucepan. Season with salt to taste.
    - Simmer the chutney over low heat, stirring occasionally, for 20-25 minutes or until the mixture thickens to your desired consistency. If the chutney becomes too thick, you can add a splash of water to adjust the consistency.
5. Cool and Store:
    - Remove the chutney from heat and let it cool to room temperature.
    - Transfer the chutney to clean, sterilized jars or containers. Seal tightly and store in the refrigerator.

Tips:

- Adjust Seasoning: Feel free to adjust the spices, vinegar, and sugar according to your taste preferences. You can make it sweeter or spicier as desired.
- Serve: Brazil Nut Chutney pairs wonderfully with cheese platters, roasted meats, sandwiches, or as a condiment with Indian dishes like samosas or dosas.
- Storage: Properly stored, Brazil Nut Chutney can last in the refrigerator for up to 2 weeks. Make sure to use clean utensils when scooping out the chutney to prevent contamination.

Enjoy this Brazil Nut Chutney as a delicious and versatile condiment that adds a unique nutty flavor to your meals!

Brazil Nut Loaf

Ingredients:

- 1 cup Brazil nuts, chopped
- 2 cups all-purpose flour
- 1 teaspoon baking powder
- 1/2 teaspoon baking soda
- 1/2 teaspoon salt
- 1/2 cup unsalted butter, softened
- 1 cup granulated sugar
- 2 large eggs
- 1 teaspoon vanilla extract
- 1 cup plain yogurt or sour cream

Instructions:

1. Preheat Oven:
   - Preheat your oven to 350°F (175°C). Grease and flour a 9x5-inch loaf pan or line it with parchment paper.
2. Prepare Brazil Nuts:
   - Chop the Brazil nuts into small pieces. You can use a food processor or chop them by hand. Set aside.
3. Mix Dry Ingredients:
   - In a medium bowl, whisk together the flour, baking powder, baking soda, and salt. Set aside.
4. Cream Butter and Sugar:
   - In a large bowl, cream together the softened butter and sugar until light and fluffy, using a hand mixer or stand mixer.
5. Add Eggs and Vanilla:
   - Beat in the eggs one at a time, ensuring each is fully incorporated before adding the next. Add the vanilla extract and mix until combined.
6. Combine Wet and Dry Ingredients:
   - Gradually add the flour mixture to the butter mixture, alternating with the yogurt (or sour cream), beginning and ending with the flour mixture. Mix until just combined.
7. Fold in Brazil Nuts:
   - Gently fold in the chopped Brazil nuts until evenly distributed throughout the batter.
8. Bake the Loaf:
   - Pour the batter into the prepared loaf pan and spread it evenly with a spatula.
   - Bake in the preheated oven for 50-60 minutes, or until a toothpick inserted into the center comes out clean or with a few moist crumbs.
9. Cool and Serve:

- Allow the Brazil Nut Loaf to cool in the pan for about 10 minutes, then remove it from the pan and transfer it to a wire rack to cool completely.

Tips:

- Variations: You can add a teaspoon of cinnamon or nutmeg to the dry ingredients for a spiced version of the loaf.
- Storage: Store the cooled Brazil Nut Loaf in an airtight container at room temperature for up to 3 days. It can also be frozen for longer storage.

Enjoy slices of this Brazil Nut Loaf for breakfast or as a snack, toasted and spread with butter or jam for added indulgence!

Brazil Nut Risotto

Ingredients:

- 1 cup Arborio rice (or any short-grain rice suitable for risotto)
- 1/2 cup Brazil nuts, finely chopped
- 4 cups vegetable or chicken broth, kept warm
- 1 small onion, finely chopped
- 2 cloves garlic, minced
- 1/2 cup dry white wine (optional)
- 2 tablespoons unsalted butter
- 1 tablespoon olive oil
- 1/2 cup grated Parmesan cheese
- Salt and pepper, to taste
- Fresh parsley or chives, chopped, for garnish

Instructions:

1. Prepare the Broth:
   - Heat the vegetable or chicken broth in a saucepan over low heat. Keep it warm while you prepare the risotto.
2. Toast the Brazil Nuts:
   - In a large skillet or frying pan, heat the olive oil over medium heat. Add the chopped Brazil nuts and toast them for 2-3 minutes, stirring frequently, until lightly browned and fragrant. Remove from the skillet and set aside.
3. Cook the Onions and Garlic:
   - In the same skillet, melt 1 tablespoon of butter over medium heat. Add the finely chopped onion and cook until softened, about 3-4 minutes. Add the minced garlic and cook for another 1 minute until fragrant.
4. Cook the Rice:
   - Add the Arborio rice to the skillet with the onions and garlic. Stir to coat the rice with the butter and cook for 1-2 minutes until the rice becomes translucent around the edges.
5. Deglaze with Wine (optional):
   - Pour in the white wine (if using) and stir constantly until it is absorbed by the rice.
6. Add the Broth:
   - Begin adding the warm broth to the rice mixture, one ladleful at a time, stirring constantly. Allow each ladleful of broth to be absorbed by the rice before adding the next. This process will take about 18-20 minutes until the rice is creamy and cooked al dente.
7. Finish the Risotto:
   - Once the rice is cooked to your desired texture (creamy but still with a slight bite), stir in the remaining tablespoon of butter, grated Parmesan cheese, and toasted Brazil nuts. Season with salt and pepper to taste.

8. Serve:
    - Remove the risotto from heat and let it rest for a minute or two.
    - Garnish with chopped fresh parsley or chives before serving.

Tips:

- Consistency: Risotto should be creamy and slightly liquidy, not stiff. Add a little more warm broth if needed to achieve the right consistency.
- Variations: You can add cooked vegetables like mushrooms or asparagus to the risotto for added flavor and texture.
- Storage: Risotto is best served immediately while creamy. Leftovers can be stored in an airtight container in the refrigerator for up to 2 days. Reheat gently on the stove with a splash of broth or water to restore creaminess.

Enjoy this Brazil Nut Risotto as a main dish or as a side alongside grilled meats or seafood. It's a comforting and indulgent dish that's perfect for special occasions!

Brazil Nut Muffins

Ingredients:

- 1 cup all-purpose flour
- 1 cup whole wheat flour
- 1/2 cup granulated sugar
- 1 tablespoon baking powder
- 1/2 teaspoon baking soda
- 1/4 teaspoon salt
- 1/2 cup unsalted butter, melted and cooled
- 1 cup plain yogurt or sour cream
- 2 large eggs
- 1 teaspoon vanilla extract
- 1 cup Brazil nuts, chopped

Instructions:

1. Preheat Oven:
    - Preheat your oven to 375°F (190°C). Line a muffin tin with paper liners or grease the muffin cups.
2. Prepare Dry Ingredients:
    - In a large bowl, whisk together the all-purpose flour, whole wheat flour, sugar, baking powder, baking soda, and salt.
3. Combine Wet Ingredients:
    - In another bowl, whisk together the melted butter, plain yogurt (or sour cream), eggs, and vanilla extract until smooth.
4. Mix Batter:
    - Pour the wet ingredients into the bowl of dry ingredients. Stir gently with a spatula until just combined. Do not overmix. The batter should be thick and slightly lumpy.
5. Add Brazil Nuts:
    - Gently fold in the chopped Brazil nuts until evenly distributed throughout the batter.
6. Fill Muffin Cups:
    - Spoon the batter into the prepared muffin cups, filling each about 3/4 full.
7. Bake Muffins:
    - Bake in the preheated oven for 18-20 minutes, or until the muffins are golden brown and a toothpick inserted into the center comes out clean.
8. Cool and Serve:
    - Remove the muffins from the oven and let them cool in the pan for 5 minutes. Then transfer them to a wire rack to cool completely.

Tips:

- Variations: You can add 1/2 cup of dried fruit (such as raisins or chopped apricots) or chocolate chips to the batter for added flavor and texture.
- Storage: Store the cooled muffins in an airtight container at room temperature for up to 3 days. They can also be frozen for longer storage. To reheat, wrap them in foil and warm in a 300°F (150°C) oven for about 10 minutes.

These Brazil Nut Muffins are perfect for breakfast or as a snack, offering a nutritious and satisfying treat with the delightful crunch of Brazil nuts in every bite. Enjoy them warm with a spread of butter or jam!

Brazil Nut Baked Apples

Ingredients:

- 4 large apples (such as Granny Smith or Honeycrisp)
- 1/2 cup Brazil nuts, chopped
- 1/4 cup brown sugar
- 1/2 teaspoon ground cinnamon
- 1/4 teaspoon ground nutmeg
- 2 tablespoons unsalted butter, melted
- 1/2 cup apple juice or apple cider
- Vanilla ice cream or whipped cream, for serving (optional)

Instructions:

1. Preheat Oven:
    - Preheat your oven to 375°F (190°C).
2. Prepare the Apples:
    - Wash the apples and core them using an apple corer or a small knife, leaving the bottom intact to create a cavity for the filling. Place the apples in a baking dish.
3. Make the Filling:
    - In a small bowl, combine the chopped Brazil nuts, brown sugar, ground cinnamon, and ground nutmeg. Mix well.
4. Stuff the Apples:
    - Stuff each cored apple with the Brazil nut filling mixture, dividing it evenly among the apples. Press the filling gently into the cavities.
5. Bake the Apples:
    - Drizzle the melted butter over the stuffed apples.
    - Pour the apple juice (or cider) into the bottom of the baking dish around the apples.
    - Cover the baking dish loosely with foil and bake in the preheated oven for 30-35 minutes, or until the apples are tender when pierced with a fork.
6. Serve:
    - Remove the foil and let the baked apples cool slightly.
    - Serve warm, drizzled with the juices from the baking dish.
    - Optionally, serve with a scoop of vanilla ice cream or a dollop of whipped cream on top.

Tips:

- Variations: You can add raisins or dried cranberries to the filling mixture for added sweetness and texture.
- Storage: Leftover baked apples can be stored in an airtight container in the refrigerator for up to 2 days. Reheat gently in the microwave or oven before serving.

Enjoy these warm and comforting Brazil Nut Baked Apples as a delightful dessert that's perfect for autumn or any time you're craving a cozy treat!

Brazil Nut Caramel Sauce

Ingredients:

- 1 cup granulated sugar
- 6 tablespoons unsalted butter, cut into pieces
- 1/2 cup heavy cream
- 1/2 cup Brazil nuts, chopped
- Pinch of salt
- 1 teaspoon vanilla extract (optional)

Instructions:

1. Toast the Brazil Nuts:
    - In a dry skillet over medium heat, toast the chopped Brazil nuts for 3-4 minutes, stirring frequently, until lightly browned and fragrant. Remove from heat and set aside.
2. Prepare Caramel Sauce:
    - In a heavy-bottomed saucepan, heat the granulated sugar over medium heat. Stir constantly with a heatproof spatula or wooden spoon until the sugar melts and turns into a smooth amber-colored liquid.
3. Add Butter and Cream:
    - Carefully add the butter to the melted sugar, stirring constantly until the butter is fully melted and incorporated. Be cautious as the mixture will bubble up.
    - Gradually pour in the heavy cream while stirring continuously. Again, be careful as the mixture will bubble vigorously.
4. Simmer and Add Nuts:
    - Reduce the heat to low and let the mixture simmer for 1-2 minutes, stirring constantly, until smooth and slightly thickened.
    - Stir in the toasted Brazil nuts and a pinch of salt. Cook for another minute, stirring occasionally, to incorporate the nuts into the sauce.
5. Finish and Serve:
    - Remove the caramel sauce from heat and stir in the vanilla extract if using.
    - Let the Brazil Nut Caramel Sauce cool slightly before serving. It will thicken further as it cools.
6. Store:
    - Transfer the caramel sauce to a heatproof jar or container. Allow it to cool completely before sealing with a lid.
    - Store in the refrigerator for up to 2 weeks. Reheat gently in the microwave or over low heat on the stove before serving.

Tips:

- Consistency: If the caramel sauce thickens too much upon cooling, you can reheat it gently with a splash of cream or milk to loosen it.

- Usage: Drizzle Brazil Nut Caramel Sauce over ice cream, cakes, pancakes, or use it as a dipping sauce for fruits like apples or strawberries.

This Brazil Nut Caramel Sauce adds a delightful nutty flavor and creamy texture to your favorite desserts, making them even more indulgent and delicious!

Brazil Nut Oatmeal

Ingredients:

- 1 cup old-fashioned rolled oats
- 2 cups water
- Pinch of salt
- 1/4 cup Brazil nuts, chopped
- 1 tablespoon honey or maple syrup (optional)
- Milk or cream, for serving (optional)
- Fresh berries or sliced bananas, for topping (optional)

Instructions:

1. Cook the Oatmeal:
     - In a saucepan, bring 2 cups of water to a boil.
     - Stir in the oats and a pinch of salt. Reduce the heat to medium-low and simmer, stirring occasionally, for about 5 minutes or until the oats are tender and the mixture has thickened to your desired consistency.
2. Toast the Brazil Nuts:
     - While the oats are cooking, toast the chopped Brazil nuts in a dry skillet over medium heat for 3-4 minutes, stirring frequently, until lightly browned and fragrant. Remove from heat and set aside.
3. Combine and Serve:
     - Once the oatmeal is cooked, stir in the toasted Brazil nuts. If desired, sweeten with honey or maple syrup to taste.
     - Serve hot, optionally topped with a splash of milk or cream and fresh berries or sliced bananas.

Tips:

- Variations: You can add a dash of cinnamon or nutmeg to the oatmeal for extra flavor. Additionally, you can stir in dried fruits such as raisins or cranberries.
- Storage: If you have leftovers, store them in an airtight container in the refrigerator for up to 3 days. Reheat gently on the stovetop or in the microwave, adding a splash of milk or water to loosen the oatmeal as needed.

Brazil Nut Oatmeal provides a satisfying and nutritious breakfast, packed with fiber, protein, and healthy fats from the nuts. Enjoy its creamy texture and nutty flavor to start your day off right!

Brazil Nut Cakes

Ingredients:

- 1 cup Brazil nuts, finely ground
- 1 cup all-purpose flour
- 1 teaspoon baking powder
- 1/2 teaspoon baking soda
- 1/4 teaspoon salt
- 1/2 cup unsalted butter, softened
- 1 cup granulated sugar
- 2 large eggs
- 1 teaspoon vanilla extract
- 1/2 cup milk

Instructions:

1. Preheat Oven and Prepare Pan:
    - Preheat your oven to 350°F (175°C). Grease and flour a muffin tin or cake pan, or line with paper liners if making cupcakes.
2. Prepare Brazil Nuts:
    - Grind the Brazil nuts finely in a food processor or blender. Make sure they are finely ground but not turned into nut butter.
3. Mix Dry Ingredients:
    - In a medium bowl, whisk together the ground Brazil nuts, all-purpose flour, baking powder, baking soda, and salt. Set aside.
4. Cream Butter and Sugar:
    - In a large bowl, cream together the softened butter and granulated sugar until light and fluffy, using a hand mixer or stand mixer.
5. Add Eggs and Vanilla:
    - Beat in the eggs one at a time, ensuring each is fully incorporated before adding the next. Add the vanilla extract and mix until combined.
6. Combine Wet and Dry Ingredients:
    - Gradually add the dry ingredients to the butter mixture, alternating with the milk, beginning and ending with the flour mixture. Mix until just combined.
7. Fill Cake Pan:
    - Pour the batter into the prepared muffin tin, cake pan, or cupcake liners, filling each about 2/3 full.
8. Bake:
    - Bake in the preheated oven for 18-20 minutes for cupcakes or 25-30 minutes for a cake, or until a toothpick inserted into the center comes out clean.
9. Cool and Serve:
    - Remove from the oven and let the cakes cool in the pan for 10 minutes before transferring them to a wire rack to cool completely.

Optional Glaze:

If desired, you can drizzle the cooled Brazil Nut Cakes with a simple glaze made from powdered sugar and milk, or decorate with whipped cream or frosting of your choice.

Tips:

- Storage: Store the cooled Brazil Nut Cakes in an airtight container at room temperature for up to 3 days, or in the refrigerator for longer freshness.
- Variations: For added texture and flavor, you can fold in chopped Brazil nuts into the batter before baking.

Enjoy these delicious Brazil Nut Cakes as a treat for dessert or a special occasion, showcasing the unique taste of Brazil nuts in every bite!

Brazil Nut Salad

Ingredients:

- 4 cups mixed salad greens (such as spinach, arugula, or lettuce)
- 1/2 cup Brazil nuts, chopped
- 1/2 cup cherry tomatoes, halved
- 1/4 cup red onion, thinly sliced
- 1/4 cup cucumber, diced
- 1/4 cup bell pepper, diced (any color)
- Optional: 1/4 cup feta cheese, crumbled
- Optional: 1/4 cup dried cranberries or raisins

For the Dressing:

- 3 tablespoons olive oil
- 1 tablespoon balsamic vinegar or red wine vinegar
- 1 teaspoon Dijon mustard
- 1 clove garlic, minced
- Salt and pepper, to taste

Instructions:

1. Prepare the Salad:
   - Wash and dry the mixed salad greens thoroughly. Tear or chop into bite-sized pieces and place in a large salad bowl.
2. Add Toppings:
   - Sprinkle the chopped Brazil nuts over the salad greens.
   - Add the halved cherry tomatoes, thinly sliced red onion, diced cucumber, diced bell pepper, and any optional ingredients (such as feta cheese and dried cranberries or raisins) to the salad bowl.
3. Make the Dressing:
   - In a small bowl or jar, whisk together the olive oil, balsamic vinegar (or red wine vinegar), Dijon mustard, minced garlic, salt, and pepper until well combined.
4. Combine and Toss:
   - Drizzle the dressing over the salad ingredients in the bowl.
   - Gently toss the salad to coat all the ingredients evenly with the dressing.
5. Serve:
   - Divide the Brazil Nut Salad onto individual plates or bowls.
   - Optionally, garnish with additional chopped Brazil nuts or feta cheese on top.

Tips:

- Variations: You can customize the salad by adding grilled chicken, shrimp, or tofu for added protein. Substitute different nuts like almonds or walnuts if desired.

- Storage: If you have leftover salad, store the salad greens and dressing separately in airtight containers in the refrigerator. Assemble just before serving to maintain freshness.

Enjoy this Brazil Nut Salad as a light and nutritious meal, perfect for lunch or as a side dish alongside grilled meats or seafood!

Brazil Nut Tiramisu

Ingredients:

- 1 cup Brazil nuts, toasted and finely ground
- 1/2 cup granulated sugar
- 4 large egg yolks
- 1/2 cup mascarpone cheese, at room temperature
- 1 cup heavy cream
- 1 teaspoon vanilla extract
- 1 cup strong brewed coffee or espresso, cooled
- 2 tablespoons coffee liqueur (such as Kahlua), optional
- 24-30 ladyfinger cookies (savoiardi)
- Cocoa powder, for dusting

Instructions:

1. Prepare the Brazil Nut Mixture:
   - In a food processor, pulse the toasted Brazil nuts until finely ground but not turned into nut butter.
   - In a heatproof bowl, whisk together the egg yolks and sugar until pale and thickened.
2. Make the Mascarpone Mixture:
   - Place the bowl over a saucepan of simmering water (double boiler). Cook, whisking constantly, until the mixture reaches 160°F (71°C) and thickens enough to coat the back of a spoon (about 5-7 minutes).
   - Remove from heat and let cool slightly.
3. Combine with Mascarpone:
   - In a separate bowl, beat the mascarpone cheese until smooth and creamy.
   - Gradually add the cooled egg yolk mixture to the mascarpone, beating until smooth and well combined.
4. Whip the Cream:
   - In another bowl, whip the heavy cream and vanilla extract until stiff peaks form.
5. Assemble the Tiramisu:
   - Combine the whipped cream with the mascarpone mixture, folding gently until fully combined and smooth.
6. Prepare Coffee Mixture:
   - In a shallow dish, mix together the cooled brewed coffee (or espresso) with the coffee liqueur (if using).
7. Layer the Tiramisu:
   - Quickly dip each ladyfinger into the coffee mixture, turning to coat both sides without soaking too much.
   - Arrange a layer of soaked ladyfingers in the bottom of a 9x13-inch baking dish or a serving dish.
8. Add Brazil Nut Mixture:

    - Spread half of the mascarpone mixture over the soaked ladyfingers, spreading evenly.
9. **Repeat Layers:**
    - Repeat with another layer of soaked ladyfingers and the remaining mascarpone mixture.
10. **Chill and Serve:**
    - Cover the Brazil Nut Tiramisu with plastic wrap and refrigerate for at least 4 hours, preferably overnight, to allow the flavors to meld and the dessert to set.
11. **Dust with Cocoa Powder:**
    - Before serving, dust the top with cocoa powder using a fine-mesh sieve.
12. **Serve:**
    - Cut into squares or scoop portions onto plates, and serve chilled.

Tips:

- Storage: Keep leftover Brazil Nut Tiramisu covered in the refrigerator for up to 3 days. The flavors may deepen over time, making it even more delicious.
- Variations: You can customize the tiramisu by adding a layer of chocolate shavings or dusting each layer of mascarpone mixture with cocoa powder for a richer chocolate flavor.

Enjoy this decadent Brazil Nut Tiramisu as a special dessert that's sure to impress with its unique nutty twist on a beloved classic!

Brazil Nut Waffles

Ingredients:

- 1 cup all-purpose flour
- 1/2 cup Brazil nuts, finely ground
- 2 tablespoons granulated sugar
- 1 tablespoon baking powder
- 1/4 teaspoon salt
- 1 cup milk
- 2 large eggs
- 4 tablespoons unsalted butter, melted
- 1 teaspoon vanilla extract

Instructions:

1. Prepare the Waffle Batter:
    - In a large bowl, whisk together the all-purpose flour, finely ground Brazil nuts, sugar, baking powder, and salt until well combined.
2. Mix Wet Ingredients:
    - In another bowl, whisk together the milk, eggs, melted butter, and vanilla extract until smooth.
3. Combine Wet and Dry Ingredients:
    - Pour the wet ingredients into the bowl of dry ingredients. Stir gently until just combined. Do not overmix; a few lumps in the batter are okay.
4. Preheat the Waffle Iron:
    - Preheat your waffle iron according to manufacturer's instructions.
5. Cook the Waffles:
    - Lightly grease the waffle iron with cooking spray or brush with melted butter.
    - Pour enough batter onto the hot waffle iron to cover the grids (amount will depend on the size of your waffle iron).
    - Close the lid and cook until the waffles are golden brown and crisp according to your preference.
6. Serve:
    - Serve the Brazil Nut Waffles warm, topped with your favorite toppings such as maple syrup, whipped cream, fresh berries, or a sprinkle of powdered sugar.

Tips:

- Toasting Brazil Nuts: For added flavor, toast the Brazil nuts in a dry skillet over medium heat for a few minutes until lightly browned and fragrant before grinding them.
- Storage: If you have leftover waffles, allow them to cool completely on a wire rack, then store in an airtight container in the refrigerator for up to 3 days. Reheat in a toaster or oven until warmed through.

- Variations: You can add a handful of chopped Brazil nuts directly into the batter for extra texture and crunch.

These Brazil Nut Waffles are sure to be a hit with their nutty flavor and fluffy texture. Enjoy them as a special breakfast or brunch treat!

Brazil Nut Bread Pudding

Ingredients:

- 6 cups day-old bread cubes (such as French bread or brioche)
- 1 cup Brazil nuts, chopped
- 4 large eggs
- 1 cup granulated sugar
- 2 cups whole milk
- 1 cup heavy cream
- 1 teaspoon vanilla extract
- 1/2 teaspoon ground cinnamon
- Pinch of salt
- Butter, for greasing the baking dish

Instructions:

1. Prepare the Bread and Nuts:
    - Preheat your oven to 350°F (175°C).
    - Grease a 9x13-inch baking dish with butter.
    - Cut the day-old bread into cubes and spread them evenly in the prepared baking dish. Sprinkle the chopped Brazil nuts over the bread cubes.
2. Make the Custard Mixture:
    - In a large bowl, whisk together the eggs and granulated sugar until well combined and slightly thickened.
    - Add the whole milk, heavy cream, vanilla extract, ground cinnamon, and a pinch of salt to the egg mixture. Whisk until everything is thoroughly combined.
3. Pour Over Bread and Nuts:
    - Pour the custard mixture evenly over the bread cubes and Brazil nuts in the baking dish. Press down gently on the bread to ensure it absorbs the custard.
4. Let It Sit:
    - Allow the bread pudding to sit for about 15-20 minutes to allow the bread to soak up the custard.
5. Bake the Bread Pudding:
    - Place the baking dish in the preheated oven and bake for 45-55 minutes, or until the top is golden brown and the custard is set. The pudding should be firm to the touch and a knife inserted into the center should come out clean.
6. Serve Warm:
    - Remove the Brazil Nut Bread Pudding from the oven and let it cool slightly.
    - Serve warm, optionally dusted with powdered sugar or topped with whipped cream or vanilla ice cream.

Tips:

- Bread Choice: Use a sturdy bread like French bread or brioche for the best texture in bread pudding.
- Nuts: You can toast the Brazil nuts lightly in a dry skillet before chopping and adding to the bread pudding for enhanced flavor.
- Storage: Leftover bread pudding can be stored covered in the refrigerator for up to 3 days. Reheat portions in the microwave or oven before serving.

Enjoy this comforting Brazil Nut Bread Pudding as a delicious dessert that's perfect for any occasion, showcasing the delightful flavor and crunch of Brazil nuts!

Brazil Nut Baked Oatmeal

Ingredients:

- 2 cups old-fashioned rolled oats
- 1/2 cup Brazil nuts, chopped
- 1 teaspoon baking powder
- 1/2 teaspoon ground cinnamon
- 1/4 teaspoon salt
- 2 cups milk (any type you prefer)
- 1/4 cup maple syrup or honey
- 2 tablespoons melted butter or coconut oil
- 1 large egg
- 1 teaspoon vanilla extract
- Optional toppings: Fresh berries, sliced bananas, yogurt, additional chopped Brazil nuts

Instructions:

1. Preheat Oven:
    - Preheat your oven to 350°F (175°C). Grease an 8x8-inch baking dish with butter or coconut oil.
2. Combine Dry Ingredients:
    - In a large bowl, mix together the rolled oats, chopped Brazil nuts, baking powder, ground cinnamon, and salt.
3. Prepare Wet Ingredients:
    - In another bowl, whisk together the milk, maple syrup (or honey), melted butter (or coconut oil), egg, and vanilla extract until well combined.
4. Combine and Bake:
    - Pour the wet ingredients over the dry ingredients in the large bowl. Stir until everything is evenly combined.
    - Pour the mixture into the prepared baking dish and spread it out evenly.
5. Bake:
    - Bake in the preheated oven for 35-40 minutes, or until the top is golden brown and the oatmeal is set.
6. Serve:
    - Remove from the oven and let it cool for a few minutes before serving.
    - Serve warm with optional toppings such as fresh berries, sliced bananas, yogurt, or additional chopped Brazil nuts.

Tips:

- Variations: Feel free to add dried fruits like raisins or cranberries, or a sprinkle of coconut flakes into the oatmeal mixture before baking for added flavor and texture.
- Storage: Leftover Brazil Nut Baked Oatmeal can be stored covered in the refrigerator for up to 4 days. Reheat portions in the microwave or oven before serving.

This Brazil Nut Baked Oatmeal makes a nutritious and satisfying breakfast or brunch option, packed with wholesome ingredients and delicious nutty flavor!

Brazil Nut Stuffed Dates

Ingredients:

- 12 Medjool dates, pitted
- 12 Brazil nuts

Optional Toppings:

- Sea salt
- Honey or maple syrup
- Melted dark chocolate

Instructions:

1. Prepare the Dates:
    - Use a small knife to make a lengthwise slit in each date to remove the pit. Be careful not to cut all the way through.
2. Stuff with Brazil Nuts:
    - Insert one Brazil nut into each date where the pit was removed. Press the date gently around the nut to secure it inside.
3. Optional Toppings:
    - Sprinkle a pinch of sea salt over the stuffed dates for a sweet and salty combination.
    - Drizzle honey or maple syrup over the dates for added sweetness.
    - Dip the stuffed dates halfway into melted dark chocolate and let them cool on parchment paper until the chocolate sets.
4. Serve:
    - Arrange the Brazil Nut Stuffed Dates on a serving platter and enjoy immediately, or store them in an airtight container in the refrigerator until ready to serve.

Tips:

- Variations: You can also use other types of nuts such as almonds or pecans for stuffing dates, depending on your preference.
- Presentation: Serve these stuffed dates as a healthy snack, appetizer, or even as part of a dessert platter for parties or gatherings.

These Brazil Nut Stuffed Dates are quick to prepare and offer a delicious blend of sweet dates and crunchy nuts, making them a delightful treat for any occasion!

Brazil Nut Trail Mix

Ingredients:

- 1 cup Brazil nuts, roughly chopped
- 1 cup almonds, whole or sliced
- 1 cup cashews
- 1 cup dried cranberries or raisins
- 1/2 cup pumpkin seeds (pepitas)
- 1/2 cup sunflower seeds
- 1/2 cup dark chocolate chips or chunks (optional)
- 1/2 teaspoon ground cinnamon (optional)
- Pinch of salt (optional)

Instructions:

1. Combine Ingredients:
    - In a large mixing bowl, combine the chopped Brazil nuts, almonds, cashews, dried cranberries or raisins, pumpkin seeds, sunflower seeds, and dark chocolate chips or chunks (if using).
2. Add Seasonings (Optional):
    - If desired, sprinkle ground cinnamon and a pinch of salt over the mixture. Toss to combine evenly.
3. Store or Serve:
    - Transfer the Brazil Nut Trail Mix to an airtight container or divide into smaller portions in zip-top bags for convenient snacking.

Tips:

- Customization: Feel free to customize the trail mix by adding other ingredients like dried apricots, dried pineapple, coconut flakes, or your favorite nuts and seeds.
- Sweeteners: If you prefer a sweeter trail mix, you can add a drizzle of honey or maple syrup and bake it in the oven at 325°F (160°C) for about 10-15 minutes, stirring occasionally, until lightly toasted.
- Portability: Pack Brazil Nut Trail Mix in individual snack-sized containers or bags for an easy grab-and-go option for hikes, road trips, or everyday snacking.

This Brazil Nut Trail Mix provides a good balance of protein, healthy fats, and carbohydrates, making it a perfect energy-boosting snack that's also deliciously satisfying! Adjust the ingredients to suit your taste preferences and enjoy the nutritious benefits of Brazil nuts along with other tasty additions.

www.ingramcontent.com/pod-product-compliance
Lightning Source LLC
LaVergne TN
LVHW081559060526
838201LV00054B/1974